# North Williston

# North Williston

## Down Depot Hill

Richard H. Allen

Foreword by J. Kevin Graffagnino

The History Press

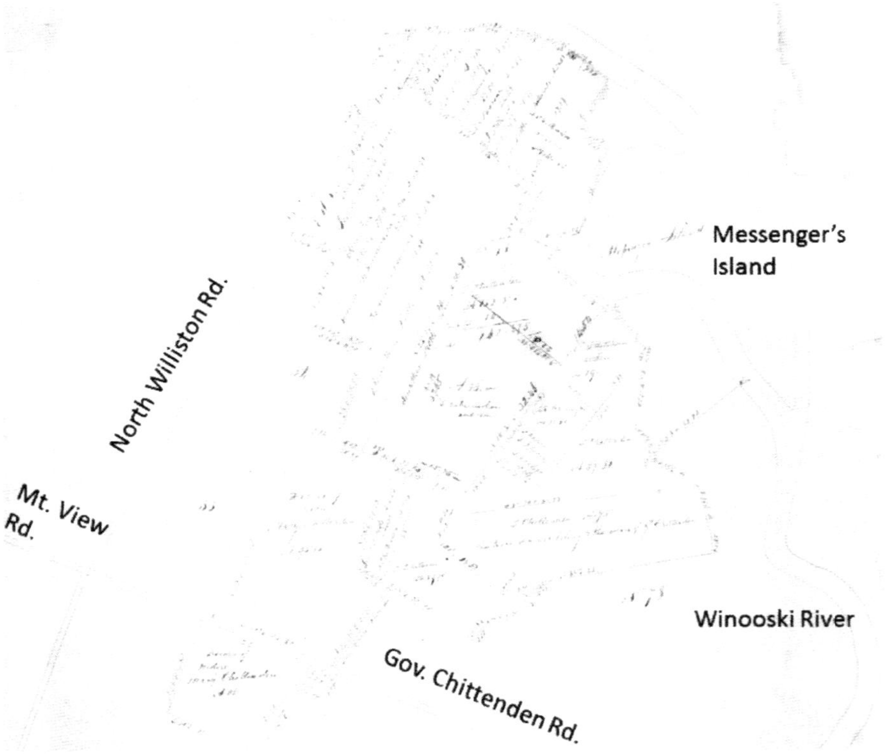


The John Johnson map of the Giles Chittenden estate, circa 1820, shows the straight route of North Williston Road and Messenger's Island. *Courtesy of University of Vermont Special Collections.*

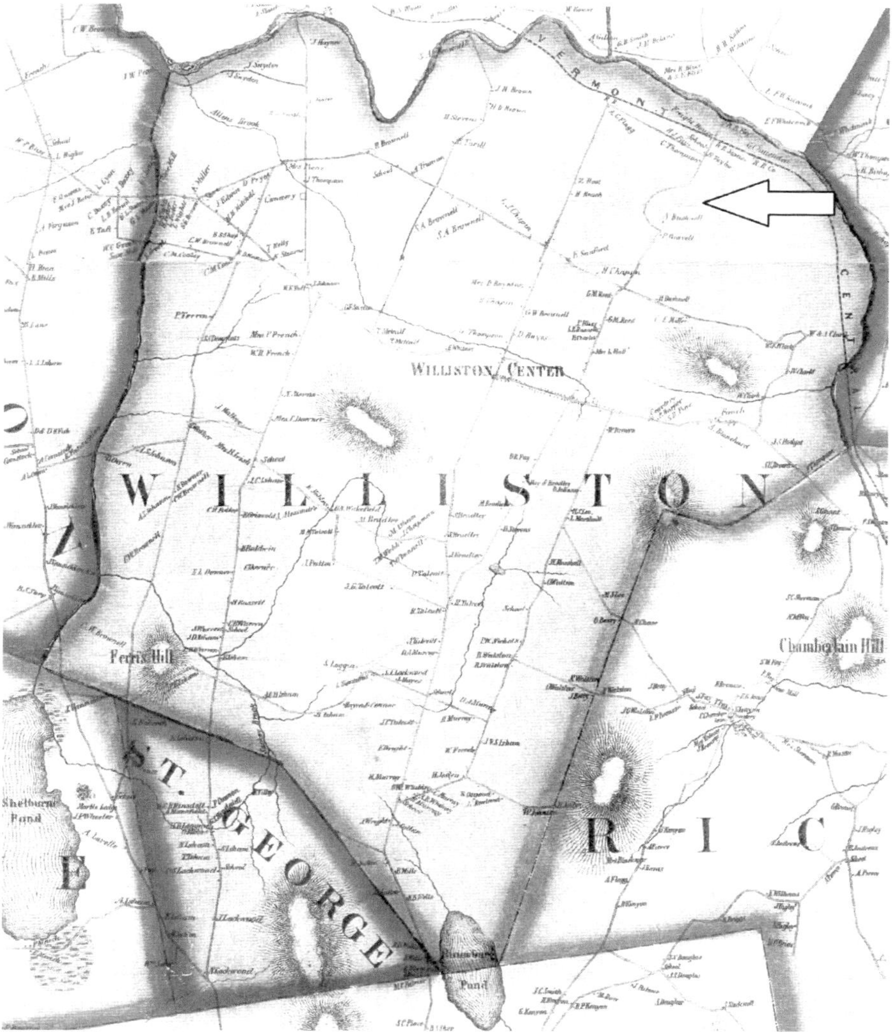


Williston from the 1857 Walling map of Chittenden County. North Williston Road appears in the upper right corner with the curve that established the present route. *Courtesy of University of Vermont Special Collections.*

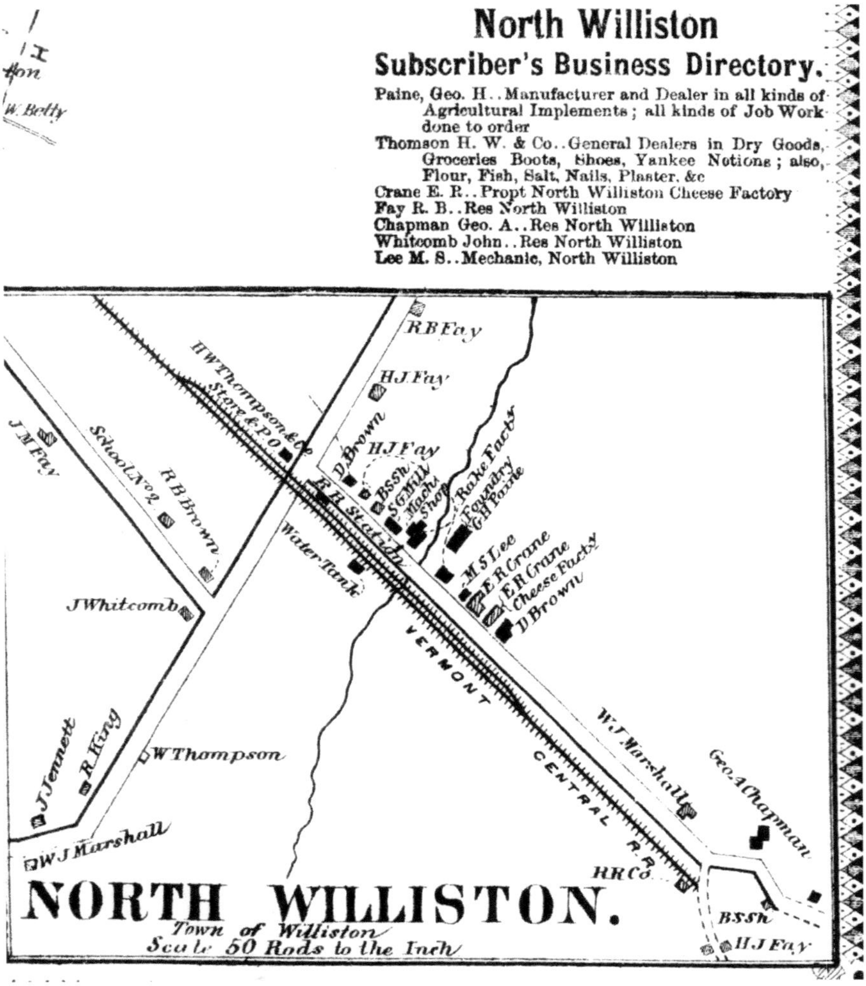


The 1869 Beers inset map of North Williston. Note the predominance of the Fay family. *Courtesy of the author.*

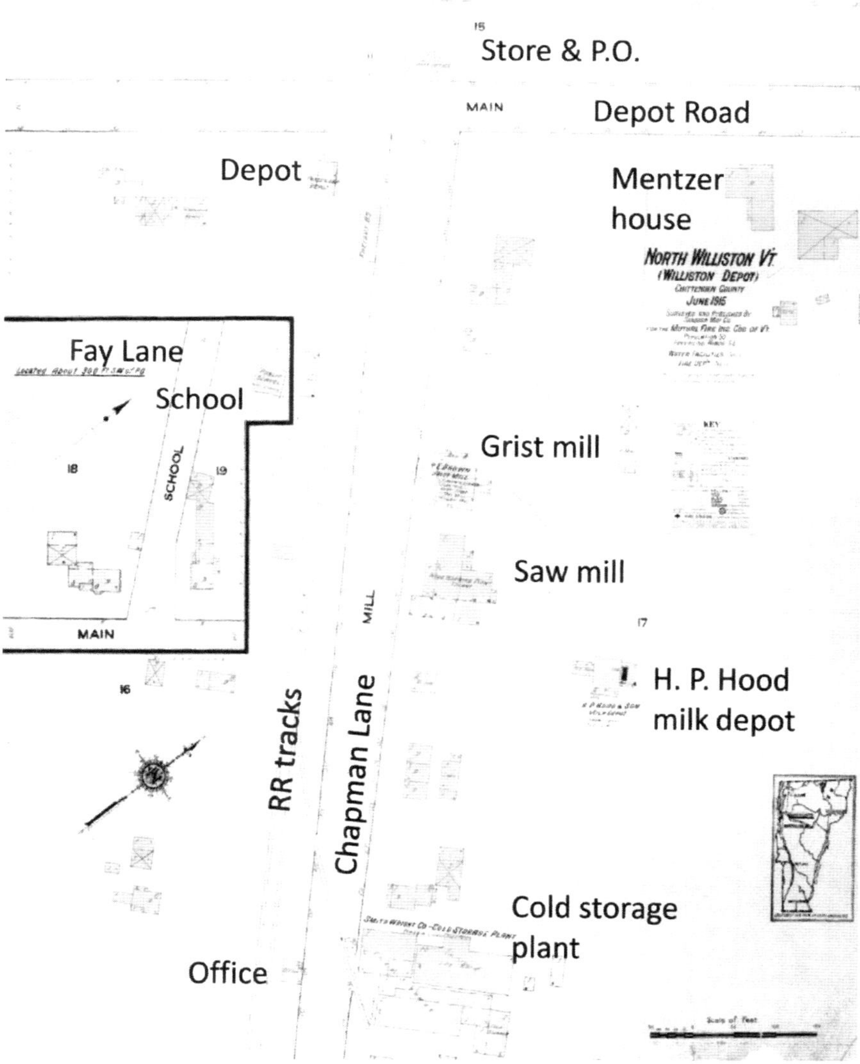


The 1915 Sanborn insurance map of North Williston locates the major industries at that time. *Courtesy of University of Vermont Special Collections.*

Published by The History Press
Charleston, SC 29403
www.historypress.net



Front cover images: *Courtesy of Julia Fifield and the Williston Historical Society.*
Back cover images: *Courtesy of Connie Chapman Dumas and the University of Vermont Special Collections.*

First published 2011

Manufactured in the United States

ISBN 978.1.60949.189.5

Library of Congress Cataloging-in-Publication Data

Allen, Richard H., 1946-
North Williston : down Depot Hill / Richard H. Allen.
p. cm.
Includes bibliographical references and index.
ISBN 978-1-60949-189-5
1. North Williston (Vt.)--History. 2. North Williston (Vt.)--Biography. I. Title.
F59.W595A44 2011
974.3'17--dc22
2011002121

*To Julia Fifield, who holds North Williston in her heart.*

# Contents

# Foreword

A famous Vermont historian once said, "Take history out of Vermont and we might as well live in New Jersey." For native and newcomer alike, the state and local historical traditions of Vermont are key components of life in the Green Mountains. People born in Vermont cherish the two-century tapestry of local events, businesses, families and industries that makes each of our 251 towns distinctive, and new residents often become the most enthusiastic members of the local historical organizations that preserve the memories of bygone days. The history that provides both individual and community senses of identity often serves as a bridge connecting old and new residents. It helps drive state and local deliberations on contemporary challenges and initiatives as well; Vermont leaders consistently outdo most of their counterparts elsewhere at remembering that knowledge of the history of any issue can help us craft better solutions and strategies for addressing it. Other states may preserve their history in respectable fashion, but the rest of America could take lessons from Vermont on how to do it better. History lives in Vermont.

The threads that make up the fabric of Vermont's heritage are the histories of our towns, villages and neighborhoods. The street or road on which we grew up, the schools we attended, what our parents did to earn a living, the teams on which we played—these are the memories that make us who we are and that drive our affection for our hometowns. This is no secret in Vermont, and it's something that has long driven local efforts to bring expatriates home. In the early 1900s, state government and dozens of Vermont communities launched Old Home Week to lure natives back, and the results are apparent today in the local libraries, town halls, churches and other structures some of the more prosperous returnees built to show their appreciation of where they grew up. That tradition continues today in dozens of Vermont cities and towns, where philanthropy to cultural heritage organizations, local history projects and historic preservation efforts helps maintain the distinctive look and feel of our state.

Richard Allen's history of North Williston is a noteworthy new contribution to Vermont's historical bibliography. The North Williston story—a small farming village that the coming of the railroad in 1849 transformed into a vibrant local economy, the decline of that prosperity in the middle decades of the twentieth century, fading memories today of railroad and industries alike—is both similar to and different from those of many other Vermont small towns. Allen ably mixes oral history, well-selected historical images and archival research into an interesting and informative narrative. Readers who grew up anywhere in small-town Vermont will find familiar details here in the stories of the pioneer generation, one-room schoolhouses, the impact of the railroad, the 1927 flood, the coming of the automobile and the growth of suburbia after the arrival of the interstate. Allen discusses these and other North Williston developments with a clear affection but also with an objectivity lacking in many town histories. The result is a book that Williston residents will cherish and Vermont historians will use for generations to come.

On a personal note, I lived in Williston for four years in the early 1970s, as a high school sophomore to college sophomore. As a sophomore at the University of Vermont, I did two unremarkable research papers on Williston and North Williston for Vermont history professor Nick Muller. There were few published sources available at the time, and much of my work consisted of cataloguing the scattered manuscript records I found in Williston church basements. A copy of my 1974 paper delineating North Williston's industrial history found its way to the Dorothy Alling Memorial Library, and there it rested until Richard Allen rediscovered it in the late 1990s. I'm pleased that my undergraduate effort proved useful to Richard, and I appreciate his generosity in extending the title of "historian" for me back to my teens, but I'm happier still that Richard has provided us with a mature and reasoned analysis of North Williston's heritage. It's an interesting and illuminating small part of Vermont's historical panorama, and those of us who care about the traditions of the Green Mountain State should be grateful to Richard for putting the history of North Williston into the picture.

J. Kevin Graffagnino
Director, William L. Clements Library
University of Michigan

*J. Kevin Graffagnino served as curator of Vermont Collections at the University of Vermont from 1978 to 1995 and executive director of the Vermont Historical Society from 2003 to 2008.*

# Acknowledgements

I have drawn upon the good graces and support of many people and organizations to put together this history of North Williston and biography of Smith Wright.

First and foremost, Julia (Mentzer) Fifield gave me access to her photos and written remembrances of her North Williston years. The hours my wife and I spent visiting her are some of the most memorable and enjoyable of our time researching local history. Julia's daughter, Ann, and her husband, Joseph Davis, were welcoming hosts when we visited Julia in Orford, New Hampshire.

James and Lucille McCullough were very generous with the Wright family papers and photos. Jim is Smith Wright's great-grandson, and the treasure of the papers yielded many insights to the cold storage business and life in Williston in the late 1800s and early 1900s. The papers are now housed in Special Collections in the Bailey/Howe Library at the University of Vermont (UVM). The family photos also added greatly to the record.

Gertrude Gonyo, current North Williston resident, was most helpful with photos, letters and remembrances. Connie Chapman Dumas provided photos and remembrances and answered numerous questions about the Chapman family. Gisele and Ellen Fontaine were a wonderful asset with their photos of the steel bridge and information on the Fontaine family. Sylvia Allen facilitated the interview with Charles Irish on his boyhood in North Williston.

I am indebted to local historian Gerald Fox, who did the research on the North Williston creamery history and other subjects. Former Vermont

Historical Society (VHS) executive director J. Kevin Graffagnino laid some important groundwork with his North Williston business chronology, which was done in 1974 while he was at UVM. I am honored that he did the foreword for this book. The staff of the Dorothy Alling Memorial Library in Williston, especially Director Marti Fiske and Assistant Director Debbie Roderer, were most gracious with their assistance.

The Williston Historical Society (WHS) board of directors—President Terry Macaig, Ginger Isham, Bob Bradish, Chris Stewart, Carol Stewart, Jon Stokes and Gilbert Myers—gave support, encouragement and financial assistance. I owe a great deal of gratitude to archivist Steve Robinson for maintaining the Williston historical records and photos, many that appear here. John Joachim shared his information on the Maple Grove Farm in Jericho.

Julie Sopher of the Shelburne Museum facilitated the permission to reproduce the Charles Heyde painting of North Williston.

Sylvia Bugbee, Prudence Doherty and Chris Burns of Special Collections at UVM patiently answered questions and located resources for me. Raj Chawla at UVM made an excellent reproduction of the Sanborn insurance map of North Williston. Thank you to Linda Evenson of the Freeborn County, Minnesota museum for fulfilling many requests for information on the Smith Wright Company in Albert Lea, Minnesota. The wonderful Vermont history collection in the Brownell Library in Essex Junction was consulted numerous times.

The Chittenden County Historical Society (CCHS) research grant funds helped with photographic reproduction. The society also granted permission to reproduce several photos that originally appeared in their publication *Look Around Essex and Williston, Vermont*, printed in 1973 by the George Little Press.

Brenda Foss of the Brockville Museum in Brockville, Ontario, and Mike Jaques of the Lanark County Genealogical Society of Perth, Ontario, supplied details on the turkey business in that area. Williston attorney Michael Harris provided legal interpretations of documents, such as property records and Smith Wright's will. James Heltz of Green Mountain Video was very helpful and generous with the reproduction to DVD of the 1990 Williston Historical Society North Williston Oral History night. Author Charles Fish shared his North Williston information and insights with me.

I am indebted to Victoria Hughes of VHS and Kay Schlueter for help with PastPerfect museum software. Robert Jones and James Murphy shared valuable railroad information. Orson Kingsley of the Henry Sheldon Museum in Middlebury, Vermont, helped with information on John W.

Wright in Addison. Jonathan Long of Jon's Darkroom & Frameshop, Inc., helped with some photo work.

Tanya Marshall, assistant state archivist, and Lisa May helped with the search for legal records on the covered bridge. Jane Talcott Mongeon helped with the identification of the Talcott photos. Joanne Riley provided valuable assistance based on her knowledge of past and present North Williston residents. Stephen and Brenda Perkins helped with the question of the original route of North Williston Road. Ronald Gauthier of Dubois & King, Inc., Consulting Engineers was a great assistance with his Williston ancient road research.

Current North Williston residents Marianne Riordan, Stephen Mease and Cheryl Dorshner aided with North Williston details. Williston town planner Jessica Andreoletti accompanied me on walks to discover the ancient roads of North Williston. The staff in the Williston town clerk's office, particularly Kathy Smardon, helped with research in town records. Nancy Rogers, Franklin County Historical Society (New York), helped with genealogical inquiries. Thank you to all of them.

My wife, Lucille, assisted with the Julia Fifield interviews and visits and editing the text; and my son, Daniel, helped with transcription of the 1990 North Williston Oral History night DVD. Daughters Elizabeth and Jill Allen also honed the manuscript with their editing expertise.

Lastly, I thank Whitney Tarella and Amber Allen at The History Press for guidance through the publication process. The support and encouragement of all these people and organizations made this an enjoyable and successful project.

# Introduction

On October 29, 1990, the Williston Historical Society held an evening meeting that was billed as an opportunity for North Williston residents, past and present, and others to share their remembrances about that section of town. The participants included James McCullough, Marvin "Bob" Chapman, Henry Tarrier, Raymond Fontaine, Gertrude Gonyo, Lucia Willard, Wesley "Red" Willard, Julia (Mentzer) Fifield and Margaret "Peg" Chapman. Howard Carpenter, president of the historical society, emceed the meeting in the Old Brick Church. For over an hour, the wonderful stories from the people poured forth. They recounted their recollections of the train depot, shopping at the general store, attending school, cutting ice for the cold storage plant, playing in the fields and woods, sliding down Depot Hill, witnessing the 1927 flood and learning how the telegraph and phone lines worked.

This was a piece of Williston history that needed to be preserved, and I knew at that time I would try to get the North Williston stories down.

Today, that tranquil rural section of Williston near the railroad tracks and the Winooski River is still known as North Williston. But it wasn't always so quiet; at one time, it was a thriving village in its own right. What made it such a vital part of Williston? Why do former and current residents remember it so fondly? What role did the floods and fires play in the transformation of North Williston?

These North Williston stories are told with material drawn from Williston town records, a wealth of Wright family papers from James and Lucille McCullough, newspaper files, the collection in the Vermont Room at the

Dorothy Alling Memorial Library and the photographs and remembrances of residents, past and present.

Before the arrival of the railroad in 1849, North Williston remained an isolated section of town with a few residents and farms. According to historian J. Kevin Graffagnino, "[B]y all logical or rational reasoning, North Williston should never have been a commercial center to begin with. It had no outstanding features, no abundant natural resources, no large population, in short, nothing to make it into a significant economic position in Chittenden County for fifteen years."

From 1849 on, North Williston gained importance along with the predominance of the railroad. The trains brought passengers, freight and the mail to Williston. Numerous industries sprang up close to the tracks. With the decline of the railroad, businesses in North Williston closed. Over the years, the area reverted to its former quiet self.

When the double-barreled covered bridge was built in 1860 to accommodate traffic in both directions simultaneously, North Williston and the rail service there became connected to the neighboring towns of Essex, Jericho and Underhill. The demise of the covered bridge by ice in April 1923 was recorded in the diaries of Paul Chapman and George Talcott and remembered in the stories of Julia Fifield and Henry Tarrier. The Winooski River also left its mark on the North Williston farms during the flood of 1927.

Today's North Williston Road has undergone some changes over the years. It has been rerouted and renamed, and it was proposed at one time to change it to a plank road.

North Williston became the industrial and commercial section of Williston from roughly 1860 to the 1930s, attracting businessmen such as Smith Wright and John Whitcomb, who used the area as a base to acquire significant wealth and influence.

Wright's ambition to become more than a small farmer and storekeeper led to a very successful business that prospered for a second generation under the proprietorship of his three sons. Locally, Wright pioneered the use of cold storage; produce was kept on ice and shipped via the railroad to the cities. His company stretched from Iowa and Minnesota, serving hotels in the Adirondacks, as well as being a major supplier of poultry, eggs and butter to the Boston and New York City markets.

Although he never lived in North Williston, Wright was responsible for much of the economic activity there. The cold storage business on his farm and near the tracks was a significant source of seasonal employment for Williston residents with poultry dressing and ice cutting. The ice was taken to the cold storage plant and used to preserve everything from antelope to turkeys.

John Whitcomb was a major figure in North Williston history. He was the storekeeper, postmaster, operator of the mill and a member of the Vermont legislature. He acquired a great deal of property in Vermont, Kansas and California.

Despite North Williston's small size, Graffagnino put it this way: "[A]t no time during its economic heyday did North Williston ever have more than twelve to fifteen homes or more than forty to forty-five inhabitants, perhaps they have a right to feel proud that their little village produced men like Smith Wright and John Whitcomb who managed to put North Williston on the map, however briefly it may have stayed there."

Other North Williston industries included a rake factory, a cheese factory, the Fay and Whitcomb lumber and grain business, a blacksmith shop, a creamery, a foundry and a machine shop.

Roswell E. Brown was a longtime owner and operator of the general store. The store was a natural center for the community, the place to gather to exchange news and gossip, pick up the mail and buy necessities.

Fifield remembers and writes about her years in North Williston with great fondness and clarity. Brown's store, the agent in the railroad depot, the cold storage plant and the neighbors were all a big part of her upbringing.

While the one-room school provided a basic education, it was also a focus point for the families with children. It was used for eighty-five years and remains as one of the few buildings still standing that was part of the boom times in North Williston.

The Chapman and Fay farms were large operations for many years, and those family names were given to the two side roads of North Williston. The Chapmans came to North Williston circa 1840, farmed the land on the banks of the Winooski River and remained a presence until 1986.

Roswell B. Fay was born in Richmond and moved to Williston in 1838. His son, John Miles Fay, and grandson, Harry M. Fay, along with some industrial enterprises, continued the family farming tradition in North Williston.

"North Williston had it all," as proud resident Bob Chapman said. The only things missing were a church and a cemetery. Those were well established in and around the village of Williston. North Williston certainly had a much greater influence on the larger area than its estimated 1915 population of fifty would suggest. Those fifty inhabitants represented only about 5 percent of the total Williston population at that time, but the economic activity was the real key to its importance. North Williston, for a time, eclipsed the village

North Williston from Bean Hill prior to 1923. Sanborn Bean owned property near this spot in the early 1800s. Two brick houses at the corner of Fay Lane and North Williston Road dominate the foreground. *Courtesy of Williston Historical Society.*

of Williston economically as the most important part of town. It rose and declined with the railroad. Once the rail service stopped, North Williston reverted to its previous character, with only the tracks, a few foundations, the remembrances of the older residents and some photographs to remind us of what it once was. The trains still pass through but no longer stop to transfer passengers and freight. Today, North Williston is a neighborhood, and it maintains its agricultural heritage.

*Chapter 1*

# Living in North Williston in the Early 1900s

Julia (Mentzer) Fifield recalls her years in North Williston with great affection. Her family moved from Massachusetts to Essex Junction, Vermont, about 1912 when she was in the second grade. Charles Mentzer, Fifield's father, worked for the Smith Wright Company in North Williston. They first lived in the Lincoln Inn at the Five Corners in Essex Junction for three months and then rented a house that Fifield describes as "perfectly terrible…perfectly hideous."

Fifield was twelve years old when her parents bought their North Williston house from Marcia W. and James E. Kennedy on May 25, 1918, for $9,000. The sale included a baby grand Steinway piano and four oriental rugs, along with twenty acres of land on the west side of North Williston Road. This would be her home until 1923, the year her father died and she graduated from Essex Junction High School.

## Julia (Mentzer) Fifield's Remembrances

*For many years we had been aware that our dear friends Uncle Jim Kennedy and Aunt Marcia were uneasy and wanted to live in a smaller home and perhaps travel. The news of their purchase of land in Essex Junction traveled fast and my father was on their doorstep ready to purchase their North Williston home. We had been guests there and knew the house well. Events moved on with unusual speed. The Kennedys built a home and moved and we were on our way to our dream home and life in the small village of North Williston.*

Close family friends of the Mentzers, such as James and Marcia Kennedy, were addressed as "Uncle" and "Aunt" because they were "shirttail relations," as Fifield calls them, not related—just good friends of the family.

> *The house was once a typical Vermont farm home, a two story, four square structure…However, we were told that in the late 1800s a fire gutted the house. The Kennedys salvaged all that was left and rebuilt in what was then considered ultra-modern, not in any way a restoration, nor was it Victorian, thank heavens. They rebuilt for comfort and not a 1900s show place.*
>
> *The highlight of our move was acquiring a fine Steinway parlor grand piano. Aunt Marcia had no room in her new home so she more than generously just left it as a gift to my father. He played by ear and loved to play. This gift was a joy for all, including our many friends.* [My father] *was extremely popular after we came to Williston. He would sit down at the piano and play any tune anyone wanted to sing.*
>
> *The years in North Williston were so perfect that it is almost impossible for me to translate it all into writings. For me life was enchanting. I was a fanciful child and a happy child. I enjoyed "grownups" and my peers, whatever their station in life, and the world around me. I was never lonely or bored. I was inquisitive almost to a fault. Before we had lived a week in our new home, a house and a collection of outbuildings and a barn, I had explored every nook and cranny.*

The Kennedy house sold to Charles and Gertrude Mentzer in 1918. *Courtesy of Julia Fifield.*

*As in most areas, when a farm is sold, the former owners leave a lot of "stuff." In our case, we bought from good friends so the "stuff" that was left was important. The barns were well equipped and ready for farming. All this made exploring true bliss.*

*I had already explored the land—ours and some that didn't belong to us, particularly a small hillside pasture. The hillside spiraled with narrow paths made by cows in search of green grass with woods beyond, all striped with small spring fed streams. When Mother found out that I had explored these lands that were not ours, I was told to seek the owner and ask his permission to be there. I did. With his permission…I often wandered over that hill and through his woods for hours. Our sole source of water was a spring on the hillside land that kept my interest. In fact, I often called this hillside my solitary playground. My friends were the small animals who lived there.*

*Each spring families of fox, mink, beaver, muskrats, and even skunks, lived in those woods and on that hillside. I often sat quietly and watched them play in the sun. I always knew right where I would find them. They all came to trust me as I trusted them. I had great trouble with the town boys and men who were trappers. After my pleading, they recognized my love and went elsewhere to do their unpleasant business.*

*In the spring, my guests were wild flowers. I coveted and tended patches of trillium, arbutus, hepaticas, squirrel corn, violets, Jack-in-the-Pulpit and many more. I would pull the leaves and grass away from the little green sprouts for the sun to help the buds to grow. I always found blooms well ahead of my school pals.*

*Mid-winter the few young* [people] *my age joined me on this hillside with our homemade jumpers. A jumper consisted of a barrel stave and a piece of carefully selected round firewood about four inches around attached to the barrel and braced to be perpendicular. A 14 x 7 board was nailed and braced on top for a seat. The barrel staves were sanded to special smoothness and waxed to insure speed. The mechanics of those jumpers was important, i.e., the height of the seat, the weight of the wood, the width of the barrel stave. There was a great rivalry in this operation. We would spend hours on end on this little hill, carrying the contraption up and sliding down again. We made jumps and dug potholes in the snow to make it more thrilling. As we got older and graduated to higher hills, this sport gave way to skiing. Jumper building occupied a lot of time. We each had many and hoped the next one would be perhaps more sturdy and faster than the last. If you had an extra supply of barrel staves, you were very popular. They were hard to come by and often expensive.*

*One spring we young came up with an idea. What about making maple syrup? The idea caught on, so we got permission to tap a few trees, but not more than four. With great care and some professional instruction, we got to work. We had good luck and the sap ran well, almost too well. We boiled in a copper wash boiler held up on stones over an open fire. After boiling all night for three nights, taking turns on the boiling detail, we gave up and plugged the trees. I will not comment on the syrup, except to say that it tasted as it should, but was very dark. The whole operation was never a repeat performance.*

A block of ice is hoisted in a lift to the upper level of the Mentzer icehouse. Another worker inside would receive the ice and pack sawdust around it. *Courtesy of Julia Fifield.*

*As a family we were very much a part of the town of Williston and we enjoyed all town affairs. My father ran for selectman and won his seat. His platform was better roads for Williston and no more potholes in mud season. He made good on his promise. He resurfaced many bad spots with river gravel and increased drainage where there had been none.*

*Supper and dances held at Universalist Hall were great. I can still smell (in my mind) the wonderful food that was served. We danced after the supper, old and young alike. Williston at its best!*

*North Williston became my world. I was, as is well known, an only child, and we were a close knit family. We worked and played as one and loved our days in North Williston.*

*We used to cut ice for Smith Wright* [Company] *at Chapman's Cove. We had an ice house at our private house, in those days. We had a walk-in refrigerator in the kitchen. You walked into part of it with a regular refrigerator door, very thick, and inside there were shelves about one foot deep, and I think there were 3 or 4 of them. There was a little bit of a door, about 20 inches wide, to the right. It went right into the ice house. That was where we kept our cream and milk. We set the milk in great big milk pans on the shelves, and then mother would take the cream off and we'd put the milk back in the cans and take it to the creamery. We still had the highest test in town because we had Jersey cows. Mother made butter sometimes and always cottage cheese.*

## Charles Mentzer's Agricultural Pursuits

Besides working for the Smith Wright Company, Charles Mentzer had corn planted for the Baxter Brothers Corn Canning Plant in Essex Junction on the plot of land across the road from the house.

Fifield remembers:

*My father broke it up into three plots. One was a pasture, one was hay, and the other one was corn. And they were rotated. We got all our seed from the Baxter Brothers and then we had specially built wagons. They were narrow with wide sides but they were deep. We picked corn, and then with a pair of horses drove over to the Baxter plant and we'd back in and unload the corn. Once or twice I was there and they were canning it…Oh, the sound, smell was very elegant…It was very fragrant corn. We loved the corn. It was a special white corn. The ears were tremendous. We brought back some*

> *of it, because we had a few pigs. I mean we brought back some of the cobs. But, of course we used the corn in stalks for the cows. But what I remember about it was, it was extra efficient and the people who had to do the canning part were always in white…It was an impressive operation.*

Not all of Mr. Mentzer's agricultural endeavors were popular with the neighbors. At one time there was some room on one of the rail cars carrying poultry from Albert Lea, Minnesota, so Mentzer had some barrels of chicken manure brought to North Williston. As soon as they arrived, they were unloaded and placed along the fence near the road to the covered bridge. It was to be spread in the spring. Evidently they stayed there a bit too long because soon a passerby stopped and threatened to have Mentzer jailed if the manure was not taken care of soon.

Julia remembers Charles Mentzer, her father:

> *He was a great guy. He was full of life. He loved to hunt birds, no big animals. He loved to fish. He knew every stream in and around Vermont after we came there to live.*
>
> *He was in the middle of everything when we went up to Williston village…The King's Daughters and the Universalist Society were always having dances at Universalist Hall, which is now the town hall…He was a good dancer. Those suppers were great. He was always organizing a Sunday picnic…the telephone would begin to buzz on a good Sunday morning. Aunt Della would be on the other end, "What could you take on a picnic?"*

Much of Fifield's life centered on the Clinton and Abbie Wright family and their only child, Julia Wright. Julia Wright, twenty months younger, was Fifield's best friend and constant playmate.

Julia Fifield's horse was named Dolly and rides in the country were common. "Julia Wright had a horse, one of their driving horses. Saturdays and Sundays and every other vacation we used to ride a lot together. I would ride up to the farm. Then we would go down to the Chapman place and around North Williston and back up again, leaving me off at home and Julia would ride home alone."

Fifield's life in the early 1900s also included many memorable summer days on Lake Champlain. The Chamberlains (family friends) and Mentzers rented a camp on the "sandy side" of Malletts Bay. In addition, the Wrights owned a camp on the east side of Coates Island in Malletts Bay that was the

The Mentzer house is 2588 North Williston Road today. *Courtesy of the author.*

Julia Fifield and Julia Wright on horseback at the Wright Farm. *Courtesy of Julia Fifield.*

From left, Charles A. Mentzer (Julia's father); Aaron Hise, plant manager from Albert Lea, Minnesota; Clayton Wright (kneeling). Standing in back: Odella (Fay) Wright, wife of Clayton; Abbie (Fay) Wright, wife of Clinton; Clinton Wright; Julia (Mentzer) Fifield; and Gertrude Mentzer (Julia's mother, sitting in front). *Courtesy of Julia Fifield.*

Julia Fifield in 2004. *Courtesy of the author.*

center of summer recreation for the Mentzers. The camp was rough with a hand pump for lake water, a long walk to a "two holer" outhouse, a small ice house and a separate sleeping building that could accommodate the three Mentzers and the Wrights. "But it was all great fun and we all loved it. We were there almost every weekend and often longer."

Julia Fifield now lives in Orford, New Hampshire, but has returned to Williston on several occasions. In October 1990, she attended the Williston Historical Society North Williston Oral History Night at the Old Brick Church. Her stories of the days in North Williston were the hit of the evening, and her participation at a North Williston history presentation twenty years later on May 22, 2010, in the same location brought the story full circle.

## Chapter 2

# Smith Wright and His Businesses

Smith Wright was one of the most influential figures in Williston in the latter half of the 1800s. He was a farmer, business man, public servant, legislator, assistant judge, county commissioner, bank president, storekeeper, postmaster and pioneer of the cold storage business in northern New England. Wright had a profound effect on life in Williston from about 1865 to his death in 1899 and beyond.

He was a prosperous farmer who granted seasonal employment for dozens of Williston residents in the slow time of the year, the winter months. He traveled extensively and expanded his business well beyond the borders of Vermont into Canada and many midwestern states. His cold storage plant in North Williston took advantage of the railroad and had no equal in the area.

Smith Wright was born to John and Polly Wright on March 8, 1823, in Williston, the second child in a family of seven sons. Smith's grandfather was Elisha Wright of Litchfield, Connecticut. Elisha was granted lots thirty-three and thirty-five in the south end of Williston, and he settled there prior to 1797. The John Wright homestead is marked on the 1857 Walling map on the west side of the present Oak Hill Road, south of the South Road intersection.

On April 25, 1844, Wright married Clarrissa A. Loggins, daughter of Sheldon and Alma (Barney) Loggins, born on April 7, 1825, in Milton, Vermont.

The Wrights' first child, Mary A., was born on July 18, 1845, and daughter Louise J. on May 8, 1847. Three other children would follow: on November 12, 1858, son Homer E., and on February 26, 1864, twins Clayton John and Clinton Smith.

John Wright, father of Smith Wright. *Courtesy of James and Lucille McCullough.*

Polly (Holt) Wright, mother of Smith Wright. *Courtesy of James and Lucille McCullough.*

Clarrissa A. (Loggins) Wright, wife of Smith Wright. *Courtesy of James and Lucille McCullough.*

Smith Wright as a young man. *Courtesy of James and Lucille McCullough.*

Like so many Vermonters in the 1800s, Wright started out as a farmer. An 1850 agricultural census of Smith Wright's farm in the neighboring town of St. George indicates that his operation had one hundred acres of improved land, fifteen "milch" cows and had produced wheat, Indian corn and oats. This property was later known as the Isham-Forbes Farm, now at 7375 Route 2A.

The biography of Smith Wright in William S. Rann's *History of Chittenden County* states that, from 1848 to 1860, he was also a traveling salesman for a mercantile house of New Haven, Connecticut. This is where he received an introduction to the behind-the-scenes operations of general stores and food distribution, experience he would draw upon later in life when he became a store owner and a major distributor of poultry, butter and eggs. Wright is credited with introducing oysters in a keg in his sales area while he worked for the New Haven firm.

Undisclosed health issues led Wright to an early retirement from the life of a salesman and a return to farming full time in 1860.

In 1865, just shy of his forty-second birthday, Wright bought Williston property from David A. Murray for $7,000. This 130-acre farm and its nearby residence were located south of the village, fairly close to his father's farm, on the road to Hinesburg. Within two years, Wright sold the farm to Charles Walston for $4,500 on October 23, 1867. The quick turnover of land, houses and businesses would become a pattern in Wright's life for the next few years. He seemed to be constantly looking for something more.

The David A. Murray house depicted on the 1857 Walling map of Chittenden County. The present address is 2480 Oak Hill Road. *Courtesy of University of Vermont Special Collections.*

## The First Store and Marriages

Wright decided to try his hand at storekeeping, so he bought the house just east of the Federated church and the general store on the southeast corner of Williston Road and Oak Hill Road from A.B. Simonds and his wife, Eliza, for $5,000 on February 11, 1868. This building would later become known as the Charles Warren store.

His account book, starting on September 8, 1869, shows the variety of merchandise he supplied for the citizens of Williston: nails, flour, tea, crackers, chewing tobacco, socks, hair pins, hinges, thread, lace, buttons, shirt fronts, kerosene and raisins. Wright's ownership of this store only lasted about two years.

On January 10, 1870, Smith's daughter, Louise J. Wright, married Ellery C. Fay. The Fay and Wright families would intermarry twice more. The twins, Clinton and Clayton, both married Fays. Clinton Smith Wright married Abbie Fay, and Clayton John Wright married Odella Fay. Odella and Abbie were cousins.

The house Wright bought in 1868. The current address is 8195 Williston Road, located just east of the Federated church. *Courtesy of the author.*

The Smith Wright store, on the southeast corner of Williston and Oak Hill Roads, was later known as the Charles Warren store; it is no longer standing. *Courtesy of Williston Historical Society.*

On March 4, 1870, Smith Wright and his wife sold the store and house across the road for $5,500.00 to E.R. Crane. As an indication of things to come, on September 21, 1870, Wright's account book lists expenses to Canada ($4.50) and a gold draft for $174.00 to buy poultry from J.M. Lanier. Poultry would become Wright's main business in the ensuing years.

## THE SECOND STORE

On March 6, 1871, "Smith Wright of St. George," as noted in the land records, bought a house on the north side of Williston Road and the brick store on the south side of the road from George and Jane Morton for $6,000.

It is not clear where the Wrights lived from March 1870 to March 1871. Since the deed states he was from St. George at the time, it is probable he went back there after selling the first house and store to E.R. Crane in 1870. Again, Wright's ownership was short lived; by 1873, he was out of the general store business for the time being, only to return later. On May 12 of that same year, Smith Wright sold the brick store to his son-in-law, Ellery Fay.

Wright became the Williston postmaster on December 5, 1872, with the post office located in the brick store. He served in this capacity until September 15, 1884.

The house at 7997 Williston Road, purchased by Smith Wright in 1871. *Courtesy of the author.*

The brick store and post office in its heyday. Smith Wright might be on the far left with hat in hand. *Courtesy of Williston Historical Society.*

Once the brick store, built around 1835, now Lyon's Apartment Building. The address is 7986 Williston Road. *Courtesy of the author.*

## ACTIVE IN THE COMMUNITY

From 1854 to 1866, Smith Wright is noted in *Walton's Vermont Register* under most of the St. George town entries. He holds positions such as selectman, lister, agent and superintendent. He also represented St. George in the state legislature from 1852 to 1853 and 1860 to 1861. In 1869 and 1870, he was assistant judge of the county court; thus, he is often addressed in correspondence as the Honorable Smith Wright.

One of Wright's earliest community contributions was bookkeeping for the reconstruction of the Williston Academy. On January 15, 1869, the two-story brick Williston Academy burned down. The fire was of suspicious origin. Carol Dean, in *The History of Schools in Williston, Vermont*, quotes the *Burlington Free Press*: "This is the third time the building has been discovered on fire lately, the second attempt being unquestionably that of an incendiary…If it is true as reported that kerosene oil was found poured on the roof and in the attic, its origin is without question. Suspicions directly point to one person."

The Williston streetscape in the early 1900s. From left, the First Universalist Church of 1860, later known as the Grange Hall, now the Town Hall; the present Town Hall Annex, built as the First Methodist Church in 1842; the original Town Hall, built in 1842 and torn down in the 1950s; the Village School, built as the third Williston Academy in 1869 with Smith Wright's bookkeeping assistance. *Courtesy of Williston Historical Society.*

Starting around May 17, 1869, Smith Wright kept a record of the materials used in the rebuilding of the academy, such as bricks, nails, lime, lumber, "sement," paint, oil, putty, flooring, shingles and door and window trimmings. He also noted the labor costs. It is not clear whether Wright's store was the conduit for all of this. If Smith Wright was not the clerk of the works for this project, he was certainly the bookkeeper.

Wright's community service also included many years acting as overseer of the poor. Vermont poor farms were established by a 1797 state law requiring each town to care for their indigent. The overseer of the poor was a town officer charged with providing assistance to those in need. In 1859, a union poor farm was formed for the towns of Essex, Williston and Shelburne, providing the needy a place to live and work. The farm was located in the very northwest corner of Williston on what is now River Cove Road.

From 1886 to 1888, Wright was a state senator from Williston. He served on the joint special committee on the Bennington Battle Monument and on several standing committees: railroads, general committee and land taxes. The senate was in session for about six weeks in the fall after the harvest and before the busy time in the poultry trade.

Williston, Vt., 188

M

In Acc't with WRIGHT & HARRIS,

DEALERS IN

Dry Goods, Boots, Shoes, Drugs & Medicines,

FINE GROCERIES, PAPER HANGINGS, STATIONERY, &c.

CASH PAID FOR BUTTER.

Tuttle & Co., Printers, Rutland, Vt.

The Wright & Harris store advertised that they carried "dry goods, boots, shoes, drugs and medicines, fine groceries, paper hangings, stationery, etc. Cash paid for butter." *Courtesy of James and Lucille McCullough.*

## STOREKEEPER AGAIN

On February 15, 1881, Wright got back into the store business when he and son-in-law Gilbert Harris purchased the brick store again, this time from Leet A. Bishop for $2,000. This was also a way for Wright to provide a business for Harris, who had married Wright's oldest daughter, Mary, in 1878. The Wright and Harris families connected again when Judith, Gilbert's daughter by his first wife, married Homer Wright in 1881.

The brick store was transferred from Smith Wright to George Pease for $2,100 on February 26, 1884. Jason Clark took over as postmaster and proprietor of the brick store.

## *Chapter 3*

# Smith Wright and His Cold Storage Buildings

The start dates of Smith Wright's cold storage buildings for poultry, eggs and butter is not clear in the historic record. Eventually, the buildings were located in North Williston on Chapman Lane near the railroad tracks, as well as at his Governor Chittenden Road farm. The North Williston buildings were sited on the lots presently occupied by 179 and 199 Chapman Lane.

On March 20, 1870, T.E. Dunlap and L.E. Dunlap entered into a $3,500 mortgage with Wright to buy the cheese factory in North Williston from Edwin R. Crane and his wife, Manora Crane, for $7,000.00. Here, Wright established his presence in North Williston on the site of his future cold storage plant. In May 1874, Wright paid L.E. Dunlap $15.00 to use the cheese factory in North Williston to store poultry. Wright probably later converted the cheese factory to cold storage.

When compared with the Wright family papers, Rann's 1886 *History of Chittenden County* is generally a reliable source on the details of Smith Wright's life. Rann states the cold storage plant in North Williston was established in 1876.

With the ownership of the brick store, we do find a record of Wright's first freezer. On March 21, 1871, Wright notes "expenses fitting up and running freezer." This included $49.70 for galvanized iron pipe and trough, $74.60 for iron pipe and $29.30 for ten barrels of salt. Lumber, labor and other expenses brought the total to $184.65.

Since the above expense listing came fifteen days after buying the brick store in Williston, can it be assumed this freezer was located there? Or was it located in North Williston, as Graffagnino noted in his North Williston business chronology?

*Walton's Registry* first lists Smith Wright in North Williston as a merchant in 1873. Hiram Carleton, in his 1903 *Genealogical and Family History of the State of Vermont,* states that Wright established "the first commercial refrigerator" at Williston in 1871 but does not say the freezer was located in North Williston.

## COLD STORAGE BUILDINGS ON THE FARM

On April 9, 1873, Wright, seeing a future in poultry distribution, purchased a farm on Governor Chittenden Road from Marilla Miller, the widow of Charles Miller, for $9,700. "It was described as '166 acres of fertile soil which supports 30 cows and other stock in proportion,'" according to *Look Around Essex and Williston, Vermont.* At last, Smith Wright settled down for longer than a few years. This was his permanent home for seventeen years until he moved to Burlington in 1890. It was known as the Wright farm and eventually became the home of twins Clinton and Clayton and their wives. It has remained in the family. Today, it is owned by James and Lucille McCullough and is the Catamount Outdoor Family Center, with about twenty miles of trails on five hundred acres. The house is one of the oldest in Williston, constructed for Governor Thomas Chittenden's son, Giles in 1796.

Wright's business was not limited to poultry processing and shipping. He was an active farmer. The 1880 agricultural census sheds some light on the value of the Wright farm. There were 30 acres tilled; 220 acres in permanent meadows, pasture and orchards; and 25 acres of woodland and forest. The farm value was $17,000. There was $400 in farm machinery and $2,300 worth of livestock. The estimated value of all farm production in 1879 was $3,251. The inventory also included 130 tons of hay and five horses.

*The Gazetteer & Business Directory of Chittenden County, Vermont for 1882–1883* described Smith Wright's buildings this way: "[They] have facilities for storing several hundred tons of poultry, meats, etc. Mr. Wright has been very successful in preserving the commodities thus stored, so that he often has goods shipped to him from distant States for storage." An 1883 company letterhead claimed a capacity of four hundred tons for these four buildings.

The Hamilton Child Company sent Smith Wright a postcard on June 3, 1882, inquiring how they should show the buildings in the *Directory*. The company included a rough sketch with four buildings, seeking Wright's

The Wright house in the early 1900s, now the McCullough residence and Catamount Outdoor Family Center at 592 Governor Chittenden Road. *Courtesy of Julia Fifield.*

This drawing of the Smith Wright buildings appeared in *The Gazetteer & Business Directory of Chittenden County, Vermont for 1882–1883* and on the company stationery.

approval for the illustration as it eventually appeared. Apparently Wright was in the process of expanding from three to four buildings. The buildings were located at the Wright farm.

With more room and land, Wright traveled to Canada to import poultry. For example, his account book shows that expenses included railroad fares, grain, nails and boards to outfit the cars to carry the poultry, a consul certificate and fees paid at St. Albans.

The prime season for poultry packing was from November to January. The dealers took advantage of the cold weather to preserve the birds. From January 12 to February 20, 1880, there is a full page in one of Wright's account books of weather records, temperature and notes on whether poultry was in or out of the building. Dressed poultry was kept outside when the temperature was cold and in the building when the temperature rose.

## COLD STORAGE PLANT IN NORTH WILLISTON

Besides his cold storage plant in North Williston, Wright also contributed to the economic importance of that part of town with the harvesting of ice from Chapman's Cove. The ice cutting represented a source of employment and income for area residents. Wright used most of the ice in his cold storage buildings both on his farm and in North Williston.

The earliest known image of the cold storage buildings in North Williston, served by a siding from the main tracks. The building on the right was probably the original cheese factory. *Courtesy of Gertrude Gonyo.*

A letter from Edward Chittenden, general freight agent of the Central Vermont Railroad, to L.A. Emerson, Esq., freight traffic manager for the Central Vermont in St. Albans, Vermont, on August 29, 1893, attests to the storage capacity of Smith Wright & Sons in North Williston and at the farm: "They have now in store 750,000 lbs. of butter, 150,000 lbs. of antelope, any quantity of eggs and I cannot remember how many thousand dozens of eggs at their storage at North Williston Depot, beside all they have up at the home farm refrigerators. They think all this could be more than doubled, and I think so too."

## Local Labor on the Wright Farm

The operation certainly offered significant seasonal employment for the local population. Wright's account books are full of details on the business.

In October 1874, Wright bought 1,169 geese, 286 turkeys and 80 ducks from J.M. Lanier for $1934.50. The business did not slow down for the holidays. The day after Christmas in 1874, 734 turkeys were dressed by thirteen people, including eleven-year-old son Clayton Wright, who dressed 6 turkeys and was paid $0.24, the same rate as the adults.

The list for January 5, 1880, of the fourteen people who slaughtered 2,268 turkeys included sons Clinton and Clayton, age fifteen, who killed 111 birds. Training for the boys started at the ground floor.

In order to please the distributors and customers in Boston, shippers like Wright had to pay close attention to the specific guidelines from *The Boston Produce Exchange Official Market Report.*

For example, the poultry had to be fattened with corn since "it is more yellow and better than that fattened on any other grain." It was worth the extra expense and would result in an increased profit.

Bleeding in the neck was the preferred way to kill poultry, especially turkeys. The birds had to be picked of feathers while the body was still warm. Details followed on dressing the birds.

When packing the poultry, the birds were to be cold, but not frozen, to avoid spoilage. The poultry had to be sorted by quality and packed closely together in boxes lined with clean paper. Boxes containing one hundred to two hundred pounds of poultry were best according to the *Market Report*.

Williston oral tradition mentions Depot Hill, part of the present North Williston Road, being white with geese as they were driven to the Wright farm for slaughter. This is corroborated by the Wright account books. On October 30, 1877, 977 geese, 630 turkeys and 172 ducks were unloaded from the rail cars and herded up the hill, a trek of just a few miles, to the farm. The "expenses (of) getting poultry from depot" were $2.

Wright's short poultry drives are reminiscent of the much longer turkey drives of the past. Before the arrival of the railroads in Vermont, turkeys were driven long distances to market. Boston was the destination for many turkeys in 1824, a journey of 250 miles, at the rate of 10 miles per day. It was economically feasible for many growers to band together and drive three thousand to four thousand turkeys en masse.

Railroads greatly reduced the need for long poultry drives. Now just local drives to and from the depot were necessary. Refrigerated cars allowed the shipping of slaughtered poultry that was ready for market. Smith Wright used refrigerated cars extensively.

The invention and improvement in refrigerated railroad cars allowed Wright and others to tap into the distant sources of poultry, egg and butter production and provide the urban areas of the east with a wider variety of food.

Oscar E. Anderson, in his detailed work *Refrigeration in America: A History of a New Technology and Its Impact*, describes two main types of refrigerated railroad cars: the brine-tank car and the ventilator car. The brine tank car was equipped with galvanized iron tanks filled with crushed ice and salt to keep the meat inside at temperatures close to freezing. The tanks cooled air as it passed over the surfaces of the produce, and layers of hair, felt and dead air space provided insulation for the cars.

In ventilator cars, air was cooled by passing through openings in tanks filled with ice. Later, ice bunkers with wooden slats were located at the ends of cars. Block ice was used in ice bunkers, making it especially conducive to shipping fruits and vegetables.

In a third type of insulated car, there were no bunkers, but just ice that was packed around the containers of food. Dressed poultry could be transported in these retrofitted standard box cars.

Ontario was a major source of poultry for Smith Wright and his brother. Histories of Smith's Falls and Perth, Ontario, claim a buyer from New York state by the name of W.J. Wright would buy poultry in those towns in the early 1860s, drive them to Brockville on the St. Lawrence River and ferry them across to some unstated destination in New York state. These histories may have been referring to Smith's brother, John W. Wright, who was in his thirties in the early 1860s. Perhaps this is where Smith got into poultry dealing because of his brother's success.

The suggestion was made by a Smith's Falls newspaper editor that it would make sense to buy the poultry slaughtered in the area and ship it out during the cold part of the winter, leading to a Christmas turkey fair that continued into the 1920s. Growers and buyers would meet and transact the necessary business. The town became famous in later years for holding the largest turkey fair in the area, and it vied with Perth and others to brag that it handled the largest volume of birds.

Smith Wright also realized the advantage of shipping slaughtered birds. In 1878, an interesting advertisement composed by Wright sheds light on what he was seeking in the way of poultry from Canada:

> *Wanted a few tons of well fattened poultry dressed in the following manner. The fowls to be shut up without feed at least 24 hours so the crops will be empty, bled in mouth or neck and picked without being scalded as soon as possible after killing care must be taken not to rub or tear them and deliver them in good order without being frozen with heads off and blood will be cleaned off the necks and drawn by cutting as little as possible leaving every thing* [sic] *in except the intestines for which the highest market price will be paid. S.W.*

Shipping of dressed poultry had several advantages over transporting live poultry, which had to be fed and tended to. The live birds could lose weight and arrive in worse condition than when they left. In addition, freight was paid on the unused portions of the live birds.

People in surrounding towns made pillows and bedding from the poultry feathers from Wright's business. In December 1874, feathers taken from 2,705 geese weighing 1,110 pounds netted $832 in revenue. Also, companies such as the American Curled Hair Company of Central Falls, Rhode Island, and H.L. Haskell & Son of Boston made mattresses and bedding. The Chicago Feather Duster Company advertised a full line of turkey feather dusters for a variety of purposes: carriage, furniture, house, hardware, piano, counter, parlor and walls. All these companies used feathers from Smith Wright's operations.

## Iowa and Minnesota: Major Sources of Produce

On May 12, 1875, Wright notes, "A.L.E. Robbins, New York, wrote me… that Cresco, Iowa and Earlsville, Iowa are places where there are large quantities of turkeys packed." This is the first mention of Iowa as a source of poultry. The state became the center of poultry shipped to North Williston

An advertisement for the Chicago Feather Duster Company from the Smith Wright papers. *Courtesy of James and Lucille McCullough.*

by rail. Smith Wright and his sons would soon spend a considerable amount of time there overseeing the procurement of poultry, butter and eggs.

The Wright family papers contain numerous correspondences among Smith Wright, sons Clinton, Clayton and Homer and his brother, John W. Wright, while traveling in Iowa towns such as Jefferson, Mount Pleasant, Morning Sun, Bassett and Washington. The family discusses the prices of poultry, impending and completed contracts and the amount of turkeys, ducks and chickens that are boxed up and ready for shipment.

In 1898, after several years of operating in numerous Iowa towns, the Smith Wright & Sons Company decided to limit their western shipping points to Albert Lea, Minnesota, located in the southern part of the state, just above the Iowa border, and Forest City, Iowa. By this time, Smith Wright himself was well out of the business, having moved to Burlington.

## John W. Wright

Smith Wright's younger brother by ten years, John Wesley Wright, was also involved in the poultry business. He was located at Chimney Point in Addison, Vermont, and had many dealings with suppliers in New York state.

John Wright is on the Addison town grand list, starting in 1869 with an eighty-seven-and-one-half-acre farm. John had married Eugenia Norton, whose father, Phineas Norton, along with John's brother, Smith Wright, helped the couple purchase the property that was known as the Benjamin Paine/Payne farm.

John Wright built a barn and cistern so his registered Jersey herd was watered inside the barn, a first in Addison. According to the *History of the Town of Addison, 1609–1976* by Erwin S. Clark, Wright also constructed "a large icehouse with a built-in refrigeration plant in the middle" of it. Dealing in slaughtered and dressed turkeys was noted as "a very successful operation."

The strained relationship between the more successful older brother Smith and the small-time operator John is sometimes reflected in John's correspondence. There are references to money loaned by Smith to help John. In addition, John's location in a small town without railroad access limited his business and made the shipping to markets more challenging.

In an April 8, 1891 letter, John writes Smith: "It seems very lonesome not to hear from you occasionally. You are the only one of my blood relations that I ever get a line from, excepting occasionaly [*sic*] a line from your boys. The poultry business has been a poor business for me this year. Have done lots of hard work and lost money, but I could not help it. Write me how much I owe you to date. I want to square it up."

The circa 1875 Victorian John Wright house still stands near the access to the new bridge across Lake Champlain in Addison.

## THE FINAL YEARS

In the winter of 1885, at the age of sixty-one, Smith Wright was still traveling in the Midwest, dealing with a twelve-night cold snap with temperatures below zero in Iowa. He writes to James W. Griffin of Minneapolis that he has been away from home for a month and a half. Wright was probably tiring from such a trying schedule, for in 1886, Smith Wright established a partnership with his three sons, and the company became Smith Wright & Sons.

Wright's wife, Clarrissa, died in 1889. With an eye toward retirement, Wright bought 179 North Prospect Street in Burlington for $5,500 in 1890. David Blow, in his *Historic Guide to Burlington Neighborhoods, Volume II*, states the brick Greek Revival house was constructed in 1850 by Thaddeus Fletcher, a merchant from Essex, Vermont. When Thaddeus died in 1871, his daughter, Mary M., and his widow, Mary L., became benefactors of the Fletcher Free Library. Later, the daughter donated $400,000 for the hospital named for her mother.

On October 4, 1893, Smith Wright deeded his three sons, Homer, Clinton and Clayton, the North Williston land and buildings "standing hereon consisting of cold storage and refrigerator buildings and appliance

Smith Wright, as shown in the 1886 Rann *History of Chittenden County*.

179 North Prospect Street in Burlington, as it appeared in October 2008. *Courtesy of the author.*

for carrying on the business," together with the land and premises assigned to Smith Wright by John Whitcomb on April 1, 1890. With the transfer of the property to his sons and the move to Burlington, Smith Wright was formally out of the cold storage business. In 1893, he married Ella Lawrence and, in 1894, became president of the Home Savings Bank. Smith Wright died in Burlington on November 26, 1899. In a page one story, the *Burlington Clipper* mourned his death:

> *Smith Wright was a man of unquestioned business integrity, the personification of honesty and a true-hearted Christian gentleman. He dealt fairly by all men. His prosperity was attained through close application to the details of different enterprises in which he was interested. He worked hard and success and the respect of his fellows crowned his efforts. No community could possess too many men like him.*

The *Burlington Free Press and Times* on November 30, 1899, gave this description of the funeral:

> *The funeral of Hon. Smith Wright was held yesterday afternoon at 1 o'clock from his late residence on North Prospect street. The house was filled with relatives and friends of the deceased, among them being trustees of the Home Savings bank, of which Mr. Wright was president, and a representative from each of the other banks in the city. Around the casket were placed beautiful floral tributes from the sons of the deceased, the trustees of the Home Savings bank and other friends. Rev. P.M. Synder officiated and Rev. J.H. Metcalf offered prayer. Two selections were rendered by the College Street church choir. The bearers were the three sons of the deceased, Homer, Clinton and Clayton Wright, and son-in-law, Gilbert Harris. The remains were taken to Williston for interment, where a large number of friends gathered at the grave for the last service.*

Smith Wright left to his wife, Ella L. Wright, the house on North Prospect Street, along with two horses and all the carriages and harnesses, and all of the household furniture and musical instruments, books and pictures. She also received one hundred shares of Merchants National Bank of Burlington.

To his daughter, Mary A. Harris, he left $4,000; to daughter Louise A. Fay, $6,000; and to son, Homer E. Wright, $4,000. ("To make him equal with what I have given my other two sons, C.J. and C.S. Wright.")

The remainder was to be divided equally between the three sons. His total estate was valued at $53,751.50.

Smith Wright was a substantial figure in Williston during the last half of the nineteenth century. His public service and wealth impacted the entire town, and his legacy was carried on after his death by his sons, Homer, Clinton and Clayton.

## *Chapter 4*

# The Company Undergoes Changes

The cold storage business continued mainly under the supervision of sons Clinton and Clayton after Smith Wright's death in 1899. The plant in North Williston was used in some capacity until it was destroyed by fire in 1934. The sons still dealt with poultry, butter and eggs, but after forty or so years of travel and tending to the details they began to explore selling the business.

The *Evening Tribune* of Albert Lea, Minnesota, describes the company this way in May 1912:

> *The mammoth business of the firm had been the outgrowth of an experiment in the poultry raising business by Smith Wright, a man of old New England stock, marked perseverance and energy who, taking to poultry raising because of ill health, won marked success in his first small endeavors and gradually built the foundation of the firm, which with his sons has been made to be a business ranking among the largest produce firms of the line in the eastern markets, with an annual business amounting to a sum in dollars that cannot be expressed in less than seven figures.*
>
> *The business of the Albert Lea branch amount to upwards of $150,000 annually and during the busy season employment is given to thirty people.*
>
> *The management of the Albert Lea and the Forest City plants is vested in A. Hise of this city, who, while in the employ of the firm for seven years, has been associated with them in a business way for over twenty-five years, bearing an intimate acquaintance with Smith Wright, now deceased and his three sons, Homer E., Clinton S., and Clayton J. Wright.*

The processing plant in Albert Lea, probably at 221 North Broadway, as listed in the 1904, 1906 and 1914 city directories. *Courtesy of Julia Fifield.*

> *For eight or nine weeks each year Mr. Clinton S. Wright visits this territory and is active in buying.*

According to the 1914 Albert Lea City Directory, the Freeborn County Creamery was located on the southwest corner of South Newton and East Pearl Streets. The creamery eventually became the Smith Wright building. Julia (Mentzer) Fifield remembers this as where the poultry was frozen. By 1918, the company is shown on a Sanborn insurance map at this location. The city directories for 1921, 1924 and 1929 list the same address.

In a hint that the Wright brothers were ready to move on at age forty-eight, Clinton wrote Aaron Hise, the manager of the Albert Lea plant, on March 21, 1912, discussing the closure of three Iowa plants but continuing their operations in Albert Lea, Minnesota, and Forest City, Iowa. Clinton asks Hise to stay on with the company, saying, "[W]e think by the time we get ready to drop the poultry and egg business you will perhaps have had enough too, and looking after our loans will give you all the business you will care for."

The discussion of the sale of the business continues in a letter dated August 30, 1912, to R.C. Plummer of Forest City, Iowa, saying, "We would not consider selling our western receiving stations without including our refrigerating plant here and our entire poultry and egg business, as they all go together to make up the entire equipment. If your customer is favorable to this proposition…would be glad to go into details and price."

Two years later, on April 27, 1914, a letter from Smith Wright & Sons to John H. Wright in Independence, Iowa, approves the sale of the Forest City plant to Independence Produce Co. for $2,000. "We ought to have more money for the place, but buyers that will pay cash are not plenty and we have decided to accept their offer." So the company could be sold in pieces after all.

In the meantime, as another source of income, the Wright brothers loaned people money for their mortgages. Aaron Hise in Albert Lea acted as an agent for the company when it came time for loan payments. In an October 8, 1913 letter to Hise, five different loans are mentioned with the urging to collect past-due payments. Hise is encouraged to make other loans. "What have you in sight for loans now?...We can use about $10,000 more in good loans."

The twins were probably interested in pursuing a more exciting and modern enterprise. Around 1911, Clayton was driving a Stevens-Duryea touring car, and *Walton's Vermont Register* from 1915 to 1924 had the following listing under the Williston merchants: "Automobiles C.J. and C.S. Wright." Apparently, the Wright brothers were dabbling in car sales.

Their interest in modernization prompted the Wright brothers to team up with Frank Talcott in 1918 to bring electricity from the transformer in North Williston, "the location of the main east–west line, to Governor Chittenden Road and North Williston Road. Soon after that, they ran a line to the Village and a short way on Route 2," according to Ruth Painter's research. In a reminder of the times, in the same news item that told of the electricity project, was this insertion: "The town schools, churches, and library are closed until further notice on account of the number of cases of influenza." The 1918 influenza pandemic was one of the most devastating to ever hit the world population, killing millions, including an estimated 675,000 Americans.

## The Smith Wright Company

On November 20, 1914, articles of association of a corporation under the name "Smith Wright Company" were filed with the Vermont secretary of state. The corporation had five hundred shares of capital stock, $100 per share

The poultry yards of the Smith Wright Company in Albert Lea, probably at the south end of Madison Avenue around 1910. *Courtesy of Julia Fifield.*

for a total price of $50,000. It was signed by Homer E., Clayton J. and Clinton S. Wright. Shortly thereafter, on November 24, the three Wright brothers transferred the North Williston property to the Smith Wright Company.

This was likely the point at which Fifield's father, Charles Mentzer, and George Chamberlain got involved with the business. Mentzer left the wholesale beef firm of W.C. and A.F. Mentzer in Boston, moved his family first to Essex Junction and later to North Williston to run the Smith Wright Company.

In the October 6, 2008 interview, Fifield states her father and George Chamberlain felt there was plenty of potential left in the Smith Wright Company.

> *My father established a product, frozen broilers…they were the little broilers beautifully packed…very carefully in these wooden boxes. He called them milk-fed broilers. He bought the small chickens and they were housed in Albert Lea in great big apartments about as tall as this room. They were fed…Quaker Oats…I don't know if it was sour milk or what it was. It was mixed so that the chickens had a mixture…There were troughs in front of them. When that was put in, those chickens ate like crazy. When it was time to be slaughtered, they were on a runway. One would come and the fellow would take the feathers, the next one would take the pin feathers, and so on, until the last one took out the entrails. Then they were…packed and*

From left, Brothers Homer and Clinton Wright and Charles Mentzer at the cold storage plant in North Williston. *Courtesy of Julia Fifield.*

> *frozen... They were frozen with ammonia. They went in a room and were frozen solid right then and there.*

Fifield remembers her visit to Albert Lea, Minnesota:

> *My father was an excellent business man too. Very easy to do business with. He traveled a great deal. Of course he was in Boston, New York, and Chicago and in Albert Lea. He was there for maybe two and a half months every year buying poultry... It was always December, January, and February. The year my mother and I went with him—we went early in*

*December and stayed all through January. We stayed at the Albert Lea Hotel. We had two rooms and a bathroom. They had a dining room, but there was also a hole-in-the-wall that was sort of connected with the hotel. It was very close to the Smith Wright Company office or plant. But the main street went down and about two streets later the plant was right there. I was only in third grade and my mother let me walk. Albert Lea was quite a city in those days. I walked down to the plant. I used to spend hours watching them do the broilers.*

Meals on the steamer *Ticonderoga*, as it traveled the waters of Lake Champlain, weren't always true to fact, according to Fifield.

*We used to furnish all the turkeys for the boats that went on Lake Champlain. And my father always had friends from Boston coming to talk business with him. He would always take them on the* Ticonderoga, *on the trip up and down the lake. We would be met at the gangplank, as you all were as you went on the boat. My father would always say, "Turkey today?"*

*"Yes suh, we took it right on the boat. Vermont turkey, took it right on the boat!"* [responded the steward.] *Of course it was raised in Albert Lea, Minnesota.*

The interior of the cold storage building in North Williston, as Fifield remembers it:

The North Williston cold storage buildings with refrigerated railroad cars. *Courtesy of Julia Fifield.*

> *There were no windows in the storage building, the walls were double thick. The upstairs was unfinished, but there had to be some light. They had a trough that went around the room. I think it was metal lined. And the pipes were about eight inches across. The chopped ice and salt filled these troughs and then the brine went down in the pipes. And the pipes in the room were covered with frost. The icing was done with a horse and one man. Two men—one up in the top of that building, and one loading the ice and the salt. That was done every single morning.*

The pipes were about eighteen inches apart and went all around the room. The ice and salt mix produced a lower temperature than that of ice alone, which was about thirty-five degrees Fahrenheit. Fifield continues, "As the barrel of ice and salt was lifted up from the ground floor, it was dumped into a cart. And the cart went around; it was just a two-wheeled cart and it had a slide in the end. And they dumped it in and filled that trough."

The set up was described this way in a March 13, 1913 letter to Swift and Company, North Market Street, Boston from Smith Wright & Sons: "We carry our egg rooms at a temperature of twenty-nine degrees, but we can carry at any temperature you may desire. We use salt and ice freezers, the containers are perpendicular tubes on the walls and are screened from the storage space. We are able to regulate the temperature and humidity perfectly and have been able to produce most satisfactory results for many years."

## Ice Harvesting for the Company

Roderick Messenger established his farm in the southwest corner of Jericho on the Onion (Winooski) River in 1774. The family name was left on a unique landform in Williston. Messinger's/Messenger's Island was a large tract of land surrounded by two channels of the river. It is clearly marked on the circa 1820 Johnson map of the Giles Chittenden estate. Eventually, the river reverted to one channel, and the now nonexistent island became much of the Chapman farm. Chapman's Cove, once part of the Winooski River that helped form Messenger's Island, was the source of the ice harvested in North Williston.

Lucia Chapman's diary entry of January 30, 1878, provides an early notation on this activity: "Marvin [W. Chapman] began to draw ice." This nineteenth-century ice harvesting was done with hand tools and horse-drawn equipment.

The field saw in action with the Chapman farm in the background. The worker leaning on the front fender might be Charles Hoag. *Courtesy of Julia Fifield.*

The invention of the field saw led to a faster and more cost-effective method of harvesting ice. Fifield remembers the one used in North Williston: "They first cut ice with a saw and then my father found a wonderful machine in Chicago that cut ice…it went on runners and it had a big arm out front with a circular saw…They would mark the rows and then they'd run this saw right along the ice and cut the ice with the saw. That was one of the first ones to come to the State of Vermont."

"When my father brought the gasoline powered ice saw into town, Charlie [Hoag] was on the doorstep to be hired to run it. My father, with some hesitation, hired him. Because the machine was lethal, my father was on hand whenever it was in use," recalls Fifield.

Hoag, according to Fifield, was told, "Of all things, do not hold the saw down. If it doesn't stay down, let it stay up," by Charles Mentzer.

"In spite of warnings, Charlie insisted on walking by the saw and pushing it deeper in the ice. My father said, 'Your pants will get caught.' It happened and Charlie almost lost his leg. After a long stay in the hospital, he returned to the Fay's for rehab."

Hoag's fate was detailed in a newspaper clipping saved in the John Forbes scrapbook in the Williston Historical Society collection:

Blocks of ice hauled out of the cove by a conveyor system. *Courtesy of Julia Fifield.*

> *"Charles Hoag Badly Cut By Ice Saw, In Serious Condition"*
> *Feb. 11, 1919*
> *Charles Hoag was cutting Tuesday for C. Mentzer and Co. with an ice cutter, when the saw caught one leg, cutting and tearing the flesh and smaller bone from the knee to his foot. He was taken to H.M. Fay's, where he boards. Dr. M. Hunter of Essex Junction was called and dressed the wounds. He was in serious condition and could not be taken to a hospital. A nurse is caring for him.*

The blocks of ice were brought up to the double runner sled on a conveyor system. The hook at the back of the block would be down in the water, attached to the block and pulled to the platform by horse power.

"They kept that platform covered with blocks of ice so when the sleigh came down, they just slid them off on to the sleigh and on up to the village. These men were busy all the time, keeping that platform full of ice," recalls Fifield.

As a child, Fifield enjoyed the spectacle of cutting ice immensely:

> *We used to ride down on the double runners that carried the ice back…then we would come back on the ice. But we had to promise…we had to play*

*by the rules. Oskar Stapel was sometimes with us. Clayton and Barbara Brown, grandchildren of Rozie's, and Donald Teachout. And once in a while some of the other boys that didn't do anything but hunt and trap most of the time. They would ride with us, but, believe me, the men that drove, they went back and forth, and back and forth all day long. Of course we got tired after a while, but we used to do a lot of that.*

## THE COMPANY'S LAST CHAPTER AND THE FIRE

In March 1923, a full-page advertisement for Smith Wright Company appeared in the *Clarion*, the Essex Junction High School newspaper. Charles A. Mentzer is listed as president and treasurer and Harry H. Teachout, secretary. The advertisement lists branches of the company in Albert Lea, Austin and Waldorf, Minnesota, as well as Northwood, Iowa. Offices were in Chicago at the Union Stock Yards and Boston at 24 South Market Street. But the headquarters are in Williston. The photo proudly displays the Albert Lea plant, the former Freeborn County Creamery. This configuration of the company reverses the 1898 decision to limit plants to Albert Lea and Forest City, Iowa.

Charles Mentzer died on May 28, 1923. Fifield was allowed to graduate from Essex Junction High School without taking the final exams. So what to do with the Smith Wright Company?

Gertrude Mentzer had been involved with the business for a good part of the year before her husband, Charles, died. He had been sick, and Gertrude had handled many of the details. Fifield recalls, "They felt, Mr. Chamberlain particularly, and he had four boys that were in business with him; Chamberlain & Company, and none of them wanted to come to Vermont. He said that it would not be right for a woman to try to run a speculative business like that."

Gertrude Mentzer soon sold her house in North Williston, and she and daughter Julia moved to the Boston area that same year.

During the annual meeting of the stockholders of Smith Wright Company on October 22, 1923, the board of directors elected George N. Chamberlain, Winthrop W. Chamberlain and Charles W. Chamberlain, all of Watertown, Massachusetts, and Henry F. Brothers and Jessie M. Brothers of Williston.

The Smith Wright Company in Albert Lea went through some changes. In January 1926, Armour & Company purchased the entire holdings of the Smith Wright Company in Albert Lea. In December of that same year, Smith Wright Company bought back the Armour plant with George Chamberlain, coming from Boston to close the deal. It is not evident what factors reversed the deal.

The Smith Wright Company was a business in Albert Lea at least until January 1929, when it was still listed in the Albert Lea telephone book. The next available phone book is July 1931, and Smith Wright is not listed.

The cold storage building remained in use in North Williston until 1934. Burlington stores would keep some products there. Ice harvesting continued on Chapman's Cove. Newspaper clippings from 1933 detail several injuries to the workers.

"Howard Mace had one foot severely injured Wednesday morning while loading ice at North Williston. A pike pole penetrated his foot, passing right through. Dr. Hunter dressed the wound. It is expected that it will be some time before he is able to work," according to the *Burlington Free Press and Times* on February 16.

"Marshal O'Brien, who was working at North Williston harvesting ice, had one hand injured with a pike pole. Dr. Hunter dressed the wound," reported the *Burlington Clipper* on March 2.

On January 12, 1934, the cold storage plant in North Williston burned to the ground. The estimated value of the loss was $10,000 to $15,000. Both the Essex Junction and Burlington fire departments fought the blaze, but there were only some smaller separate buildings to save by the time they arrived. The Burlington fire department had received a call at 4:46 a.m., but icy roads impeded their travel to North Williston.

Emilie Stapel, who lived across the tracks from the cold storage plant, remembers it this way. "It was 4:00 a.m. and I heard a car tooting its horn. I thought it was for me since I was a nurse. I jumped out of bed and saw the whole sky was red. It was that fire across the tracks. It was quite a fire and quite a loss for North Williston."

State fire marshal A.G. Preble was unable to say for sure what started the fire in the building owned by the Chamberlain Company of Boston and under the operation of K.D. Smith and several others from St. Albans. At the time of the fire, it was being used to store apples and winter squash.

Shortly after the fire, Oskar Stapel, Emilie's husband, wrote a letter to the Chamberlain Company, expressing regret for its loss and concern for the remains from the fire, which he called "dangerous as well as unsightly." He inquired about purchasing the lot or getting paid to clean it up.

George Chamberlain replied, "I have your letter of February 12, regarding the land that we own at North Williston. If you are interested in this land

The office building for the cold storage plant as it appeared in 1972 at the McCullough residence on Governor Chittenden Road. *Courtesy of the Chittenden County Historical Society and the University of Vermont Special Collections.*

and will submit a bid of what you think it is worth to you, we shall be very glad to try to do business with you, as we have no further use for the land."

Stapel made the following offer: "You asked me to submit a bid on this land. In view of the expense of clearing away a very large amount of tin, slate and other debris, before this property can be used for anything, I have reached the conclusion that it is not worth over fifty dollars ($50.00)."

On March 20, 1934, the property was transferred to Oskar Stapel, and in October of that year, the stockholders of the Smith Wright Company voted to dissolve the corporation.

The North Williston cold storage plant had an office building located near the main line of the tracks. After the 1934 fire destroyed the storage buildings, the office was moved to the Wright farm. During the 1990 North Williston Oral History Night, it was recalled "they shoed the building and just dragged it" with tractors, but they couldn't get it all the way to the top of Depot Hill without the help of several teams of horses. The teams had been

The foundation of the office building in April 2010, a visible reminder of the North Williston cold storage plant. *Courtesy of the author.*

drawing milk down to the creamery and were put to work as they returned to the top of the hill, remembers Henry Tarrier. The building stands today near the McCullough house and has been converted to a residence, now 630 Governor Chittenden Road.

That was the official end to one of Williston's most unusual business enterprises, which began with Smith Wright around 1871, spread to Iowa and Minnesota, served farmers and hotels throughout New England and New York and furnished tons of poultry, butter and eggs to the major distributors in Boston and New York City.

## *Chapter 5*

# The Railroad and Depot for the "High City of Williston"

The character of Williston, especially North Williston, changed greatly when the Vermont Central Railroad came through in 1849. The rail service made travel and mail delivery more efficient. More importantly, agricultural goods were shipped to markets farther away. The Williston center of commerce shifted from the village on the Winooski Turnpike to the area around the tracks.

A November 17, 1860 letter from "E.W." of Williston to the *Daily Free Press* in Burlington puts it this way:

> *Since the completion of the Rail Road, which diverted the entire amount of teaming and travel from the old beaten track of the turnpike and, consequently, from our village to the river valley, on the northern extremity of our town, we have been styled by our more aspiring, and as they think, more fortunate neighbors, "the High City of Williston."*

The railroad led to the establishment of businesses and support services in North Williston: a blacksmith shop, a rake factory, a creamery, a store and post office, a freight house and eventually several sidings to serve industries such as the gristmill and the Smith Wright cold storage plant.

The impact of the railroad was also felt in the change in the type of farming done in Williston. Holman Drew Jordan, in his dissertation *Ten Vermont Towns: Social and Economic Characteristics, 1850–1870*, asserts that

> *the railroad brought new economic life, particularly with new industries in North Williston, on both the railway and the Winooski River. Specialization*

> *came to agriculture, and milk cows replaced sheep. The number of farms and farm size tended to increase, and more hay was raised to feed, by 1870, nearly double the number of cows. Larger herds were used to produce more butter and more than a third of a million gallons of milk, annually, most of which went to two new and growing cheese factories. Williston benefited by the coming of the railroad, despite the fact its population declined, because the economic adjustments made greater profits and wealth possible.*

One of those cheese factories was in North Williston; the other was on Oak Hill, built in 1870 by Hiram Walston, which was managed and later owned by Lewis H. Talcott. The Oak Hill cheese factory put out 150,000 pounds of cheese and 60,000 pounds of butter each year in 1885 and 1886.

The diary entries of Talcott depict the variety of farm products shipped by rail from Williston. Talcott (1836–1910) was one of Williston's most prominent farmers. He started on the family farm on Oak Hill, spent some time in the San Francisco area and purchased his farm—current address 320 North Williston Road—in 1876.

On September 23, 1853, he made this entry: "finished digging [potatoes] and drawed 3 load (*sic*) to the depot. 46 bushels, 25 cts per bushel."

In 1860, Talcott noted the following:

> *Friday, March 23: In the morning went onto the hill got some potatoes and three tubs of butter that was left there through the winter, carried them to the depot in the afternoon, worked in the sugar works some and visited some.*
>
> *April 4, Wed: Bored sugar works over in forenoon, carried sugar down to H. Fay in afternoon went to depot & weighed it, had 147 lbs. in evening went to band meeting.*
>
> *October 9, Tuesday, went to the depot in the forenoon with 18 boxes cheese & 1 tub of butter afternoon fixed garden fence in evening went to the ladies fair.*

Apparently Talcott knew how to balance work and fun.

## The Depot

The North Williston depot was built in 1867, twenty feet by forty feet and constructed of brick. The building had four rooms: a waiting area, a station agent's office and separate spaces for baggage and small freight, recalls Julia

The depot, circa 1910. The numbers on the Williston sign indicate the mileage to the north and south end of the Central Vermont tracks: the 71.5 is to St. Johns, Quebec, and the 106 is to Windsor, Vermont. *Courtesy of Williston Historical Society.*

(Mentzer) Fifield. The sparse interior had varnished walls, wooden benches and was kept neat and clean. Heat came from a small stove in the middle of the building. The brick depot was situated south of the tracks adjacent to North Williston Road.

Fifield, class of 1923, traveled to high school in Essex Junction by horse or rail.

> *Horseback was my usual form of transportation, except when the weather was cold, rainy, or very deep in snow…Mother would get me ready to go, and I'd walk up, and I…somehow never knew when the train was going to be awfully late. Sometimes I came home, but very often I didn't. I'd spend an hour in the railroad station waiting for the train, and keeping track of where it was over the telegraph. The station was only one hundred yards from home, but waiting for a late train was more interesting at the station than at home.*

Charles Irish, son of store clerk George Irish, had a favorite destination: the Champlain Valley Fair in Essex Junction. A ticket would cost him eleven cents.

Fifield fondly remembers station agent Walter Fiske as one of the people who gave North Williston its charm. He was meticulous in his upkeep of the depot, and he had a rather unusual style of dress. "[He] always wore a western hat and western boots, and I hadn't a clue where he lived, but he did not live in North Williston…And he was apt to wear pants with chaps on the sides. He was a big macho guy and he always was throwing his weight around North Williston, I can tell you. Everybody had to toe the mark when they went to the station."

Fiske educated Fifield about his job. Patiently, he taught her about the railroads, the language, the codes and "how to translate telegraphy and how to use the dot/dash instrument."

Not all of Fifield's memories of the depot are happy ones.

> *There is a somewhat sad reason for my need to write about the station. When my adored father died, his body was taken to Massachusetts for burial. When this became known to my father's friend, Mr. Smith, the then President of the Central Vermont Railroad, he made all the arrangements for my mother. He had the through train, the Montrealer, stop in Williston at midnight to pick up my father's body and to take Mother and me. He was determined also to send his private car, but Mother begged him to let us travel in the sleeping car. He did insist on the private drawing room for us. That night many dear friends gathered in North Williston to see us off. Thus my nostalgia for a little Red Railroad station.*

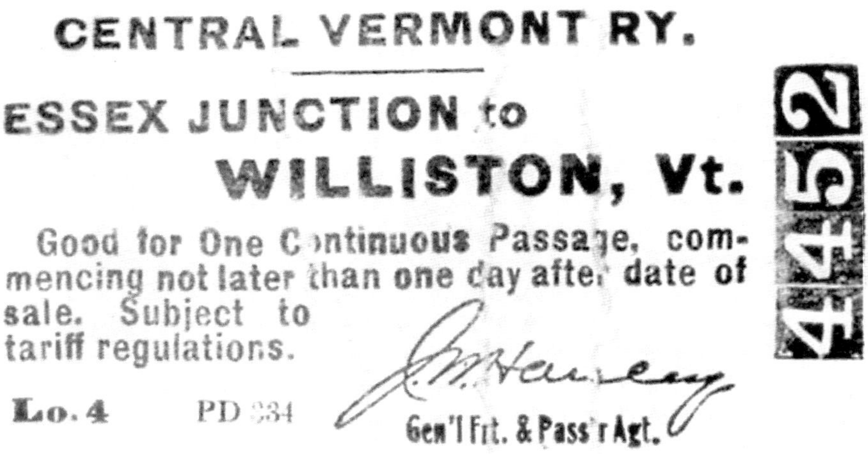
CENTRAL VERMONT RY.

ESSEX JUNCTION to

WILLISTON, Vt.

Good for One Continuous Passage, commencing not later than one day after date of sale. Subject to tariff regulations.

Lo. 4 PD 334

Gen'l Frt. & Pass'r Agt.

4452

A train ticket allowed Julia Fifield passage from Essex Junction to Williston. *Courtesy of Julia Fifield.*

When the covered bridge across the Winooski River at North Williston was completed in 1860, it created an easier access to the rail connection for neighboring towns. Farmers and residents of Essex, Jericho and Underhill also benefitted.

The 1916 history of Jericho states that there was hardly a part of that town that was too far from a depot because stations existed in Underhill, Richmond, Jericho and North Williston. All of these depots afforded "shipping points" that were "first-class." Besides the North Williston depot, the neighboring towns were serviced by the Burlington and Lamoille Railroad, completed in 1877, as it ran from Burlington to Cambridge. It was possible to have many thriving depots within a relatively small area in the days before cars and trucks took over transporting goods and people.

Although Williston never gained fame as a resort for tourists, a summer homes brochure of 1901, put out by the Central Vermont Railway, advertised the accommodations at the Maple Grove Farm of Edgar L. Barber as a destination from North Williston. It was "situated among the Green Mountains at an elevation of 1500 feet above the sea." That was a bit of overstatement. The Barber farm was and is actually in Jericho and stands at about 500 feet above sea level.

## The Stage Line

The arrival of the railroad in Williston prompted the establishment of a stage line in town. Stage service connected the village of Williston to the North Williston depot, a journey of thirty minutes at a speed of five miles per hour. The *Gazetteer and Business Directory of Chittenden County, 1882–1883* described it as a run of two and one-half miles leaving Williston daily, "twelve times per week…except Sunday, at 7 a.m., and 4 p.m., arriving at North Williston by 7:30 a.m., and 4:30 p.m.; leaves North Williston at 8:30 a.m., and 5:30 p.m., arriving at Williston by 9 a.m., and 6 p.m. H.L. Charles is mail carrier, the stage accommodating passengers. Telegrams and express matter should be sent to North Williston." The stage service was also noted in *Walton's Vermont Register* from the 1915 edition right up to 1930–1931.

The stage also serviced a section of Williston, known as Talcott or Talcottville, which was centered on Old Creamery Road near Oak Hill Road. There was a general store, school, Hiram Walston's creamery and a post office (1897–1903) located there.

The depot from the south. The freight building is visible across the tracks in the center. The gristmill is the two-story building to the right, and the milk storage building is on the far right. *Courtesy of Gertrude Gonyo.*

Fifield remembers the stage as a horse drawn wagon with two seats. She described it as a "democrat," an open wagon with iron wheels, not rubber. It was sometimes pulled with two horses, usually one.

Fifield's favorite story of the stage concerns two young women who arrived from the University of Vermont to practice teach in town. One woman asked the gentleman driver why the railroad station was so far from Williston. His deliberate answer was, "The damn fool who built the station wanted it near the railroad." The young women did not laugh—they were too naïve or young to understand country humor.

Williston researcher Ruth Painter notes, as an alternative to the stage service, "Residents who grew up in North Williston remember walking to and from the village to attend church."

North Williston residents recall observing the methods of communication between the trains and the depot.

Fifield describes a train order hoop this way:

> *a long bamboo pole about 5' long bent to make a wide loop on one end and a heavy metal snap at the base of the loop. This delivered orders to an engineer. At a signal from the rooftop semaphore, the train slowed down. Walter* [Fiske] *slipped the loop over the outstretched arm of the engineer who extracted his orders from the snap, tossed the bamboo rod*

*out onto the platform and was off. My job was to run and pick up the rod—idiot's delight!*

Henry Tarrier says: "But there were always two. The engineer got one and then the conductor that rode the caboose got the other."

## Flood of 1927 and the Railroad

The residents vividly recall the devastating November flood of 1927, although it caused less damage in Williston when compared with towns farther upstream such as Bolton.

Bob Chapman was ten years old at the time.

> *The first I remember of that was, gosh, I heard this heck of a commotion and I looked out and men were taking the cows out, and the water was way up on the lawn. They drove the cows up across the tracks. You could hear the apples bobbing on the ceiling underneath the cellar floor; floating around in there. And then there were three men, they each had quite a few children, and we waded out of the houses and went up the railroad tracks. There was water on both sides of the tracks. Went up to Mabel Brown's, I remember sitting there and watching all this stuff going down the river. One house we saw go down was on fire. It was just one barn and house after another.*

Lucia (Chapman) Willard, Bob's sister, recalls, "We were wading out, the water was up to our knees, and this barn door went floating by. And there was a cat sitting on it. I ran and grabbed the cat and rescued it."

Bob Chapman credits station agent Charlie O'Brien with saving lives:

> *Charlie O'Brien was the station manager. And he got a call from Waterbury, and the station agent there said he was standing on his desk, and the water was up to the top of the desk, this was his last message, and he was leaving. So Charlie got on the phone and he notified everyone he could up and down the valley. And his brother-in-law, who was Raymond Pratt, said "Yeah, yeah, we got a lot of those." So he turned the lights off and went back to bed.* [Charlie O'Brien] *called him back again and said "This is no ordinary flood, get out of there." He probably did save some lives.*

Damage to the railroad tracks near the Clark farm in the northeastern part of Williston after the 1927 flood. *Courtesy of Williston Historical Society.*

Bob Chapman's daughter, Connie Chapman Dumas, states that, "Dad always said the tracks looked like twisted pretzels. The old barn had a 1927 high water mark that Dad always kept painted. It seemed like it was some twenty to thirty feet up from the lowest level of the barn."

The November 25 *Burlington Free Press* reports that the greatest death toll in North Williston from the 1927 flood came several weeks after the water had receded. A train, returning from Richmond to Williston with a work crew that had been laying down ballast, collided with empty ballast cars of another train. The caboose, with fifteen men inside, caught fire. Three were killed and others were severely injured.

So what happened to the depot and when was it torn down?

"The agency was closed there on February 3, 1930," according to railroad expert Jim Murphy. During the 1930s, a caretaker was on duty when certain trains stopped. A. Muir is recorded on the Central Vermont Railroad payroll in that role from July 1933 to June 1935.

After the trains ceased regular service to North Williston, it became a flag stop where one had to signal for the train to stop. North Williston resident Emilie Stapel tells the story of her brother who wanted to have the train stop after it was no longer a flag stop. The conductor said it would cost ten dollars to bring the train to a halt in North Williston. Emilie's brother offered to pay the money so he wouldn't have to call someone to come get him in Essex Junction. But the conductor refused to stop the train.

From left, James Kennedy, Clinton Wright, Frank Talcott, Clayton Wright, Bob Leet, Homer Wright and Harry Fay at the North Williston Depot. *Courtesy of Williston Historical Society, Talcott album.*

The property was sold to a J.A. LaFrance on May 31, 1942. In 1982, Arthur Germaine wrote to the *Burlington Free Press* with this story: "My uncle, Joseph LaFrance, lifetime resident of Williston, worked for the railroad for years and retired there. He bought the old station. It was put up for bid and he was the highest bidder. The building had to be taken down and cleaned up…He later sold all the lumber, beams and slate to individuals. He also found a few Indian head coins in dismantling."

The scene that ensued when trains made a stop in North Williston was hectic and exciting since the general store and the depot were located across the road from each other. North Williston Road was blocked while the train paused at the depot. Passengers could make their way to the store for some shopping and talking. The noise of the engine made conversations difficult, as the steam and smoke billowed into the sky. The stage loaded passengers; the milk cans, mail bags and freight were transferred on and off the train; and the busy intersection would eventually quiet down until the next train, when the routine was repeated.

Today, the trains still pass through North Williston, but the sidings are gone. The Amtrak train comes through town twice a day, seven days a week, on its way to and from St. Albans and Washington, D.C.

*Chapter 6*

# The Bridges of North Williston

Ferry service existed across the Winooski River at North Williston prior to the bridge constructed to connect Williston with northern towns. In 1832, the service known as Thomson's Ferry was located on what became Chapman land. By 1836, however, there is reference in town records to Chittenden's Ferry, located at the eventual site of the bridge.

The completion of the railroad through North Williston in 1849 revealed the inadequacy of what had become Fay's Ferry (formerly Chittenden's) as a means of access to the new form of transportation for the people of Jericho, Underhill and Essex. As early as 1852, Jericho and Underhill debated increasing taxes to pay for a North Williston bridge. Soon the towns formed a joint committee to resolve the issue of whether to build a bridge and where it should be located. A proposed alternate location was at the point where the Jericho Center Road (now the Skunk Hollow Road) meets the River Road, near the Watrous Thomson house. A Chittenden County Court committee heard arguments for placement of the bridge at both locations and voted in favor of the Fay's Ferry site. Williston, Essex, Underhill and Jericho agreed to pay jointly for the project.

The 1963 history of Jericho gives this description of the covered bridge and its construction. It had a Burr arch configuration that consisted of a wooden arch combined with a multiple kingpost truss to increase the stiffness of the bridge. The double-lane, or double-barreled, bridge was about 368 feet in length with two spans and a center pier. The builder was a man named Eggleston who moved his family and equipment to the bank of the river to work on it. The final bill for Jericho was $1,400; for Underhill, $400;

The covered bridge that spanned the Winooski River in North Williston. *Courtesy of Williston Historical Society.*

The double-lane bridge, built to accommodate traffic in both directions, indicates how important the crossing was to area farmers and merchants. *Courtesy of Williston Historical Society.*

Essex, $1,400; and $2,790 for Williston. It was completed in 1860 for a total of $5,990, with a $200 accounting error.

For a present-day comparison of the size of this bridge, the double-lane bridge at Shelburne Museum, moved from Cambridge, Vermont, is 168 feet long.

The Williston town reports from the late 1800s and early 1900s mention bridge maintenance with costs shared with the other towns: new planks, labor, team work and snowing the bridge (bringing snow onto the bridge to make it easier for sleighs to cross). In 1902, this latter process cost four dollars.

In 1893, over $100.00 was spent on bridge repair, with Essex and Jericho sharing in the cost. In 1909, H.O. Ward was paid $87.40 for planking, and B.F. Brown received $100.00 for shingling.

Perhaps 1917 was one of the more intensive years for upkeep. Teams of horses worked eleven and one-half days at $4.00 to equal $46.00. Also, men labored for thirty days to add $52.69 to the cost.

Since the insides of covered bridges were often used to post advertisements for things such as patent medicine and the upcoming arrival of the circus, they could be very informative and entertaining places to stop.

But for one young lady, Julia (Mentzer) Fifield, the North Williston bridge, with all its posters, created a unique challenge:

> *I used to ride my horse back and forth to Essex Junction to school. They used to put advertisements in the covered bridge. The wind would go through the covered bridge and it would flap the papers. I had a hard time getting my horse through the covered bridge so every Saturday I would spend some time tearing the advertisements off so the horse would go through the bridge.*

## Ice Jam: "Some Exciting Day"

The bridge served the surrounding towns well until Saturday, April 7, 1923. In early April, the *Burlington Free Press* reported that, with the spring runoff, Montpelier and Middlesex were hit with the "worst ice jam in 40 years," causing the river to overflow and flood roads and fields. The thaw and ice jams impacted the North Williston bridge further downstream.

Here are two eyewitness accounts. Fifield recalls:

> *I was standing on Rozie Brown's* [store] *front porch and somebody said, "I think the bridge is going." We all immediately turned to the bridge and as we did the bridge lifted up and just laid right over…There was a man that*

> *lived there by the name of Sidney Warren.* [He] *came down the street. He was a very elderly gentleman with a long white beard...and he said, "Well, the bridge has gone out...but the side I shingled ain't moved a shingle."*

North Williston resident Sidney Warren was listed in the 1882–1883 *Gazetteer and Business Directory of Chittenden County* as a carpenter and joiner, someone who specialized in window and door frames. Through the years he also made grain measures, oil can jackets and butter boxes. Born on January 11, 1839, Warren would have been twenty-one years old when the first shingles went on the bridge and eighty-four when the ice took out the bridge.

Henry Tarrier remembers it this way:

> *My father was drawing milk to that creamery down there...They would put feed bags on the horses and let them eat down there. We walked down to the bridge, I was just a kid, and I walked down with him. And we watched the ice. We looked down; the ice was probably five feet below the bridge. And there was a row of willows on the other side. The ice started building against them willows. And then they see a big elm tree coming down, with the roots sticking up. The roots stopped against the bridge. Because all the ice was banked up, in no time at all, the water had raised up and lifted that bridge off.*

Nineteen-year-old Williston resident George S. Talcott recorded this in his diary on April 7, 1923: "Helped with chores and milking. Worked on wireless all A.M. Went down to North Williston to see big covered bridge go out. 320' span. Followed it down to railroad bridge near Essex."

Lucian Paul Chapman's diary entry for that day: "Ice going out. The big covered bridge across the river went out with the flood. Biggest loss that Williston ever had I think. The bridge broke in 3 pieces at the R.R. bridge and is hung up above Essex. Some exciting day."

The *Free Press* states the bridge's journey started around 12:30 p.m. and reached speeds of four or five miles per hour. The description continues:

> *When it came to the meadow of the Fay farm it settled there for about an hour. Meanwhile W.W. Workman, highway commissioner, had sent a telephone message to the railway company headquarters to rush dynamite and men to the scene as it was feared that the railway bridge would not be high enough for the highway structure to pass under. It was thought that it would become necessary to blow the structure up before it would reach the railway bridge.*

The April flood and ice that carried away the covered bridge hit the entire Winooski River Valley. *Courtesy of Williston Historical Society.*

> *Finally it started on again. Then it bumped against the big abutments of the railway bridge. Meanwhile an approaching train had stopped to await the outcome of the impact.*
>
> *But the old highway bridge broke in two parts and proceeded on down the river having done no damage to the high railway bridge, under which it easily passed. The Central Vermont sent men to the scene and there was a great crowd of spectators lining the banks of the river all the afternoon.*

The fate of the bridge remained a topic in the *Free Press* for several more days.

> *"Part of Bridge Moves Down River To Dam"*
>
> *A section of about 40 feet in length of the North Williston bridge that was washed away by the ice jam Saturday and was apparently moored on the river bank a mile from its original location early today floated down the river to the site of the new 50-foot dam. There it is anchored on the Williston side of the river against the great pillar of concrete, partly in the mud, and is so sunk in that one can reach the roof of the structure, the water receding during today and Sunday.*

*It is more than likely that it will have to be torn down. The larger section of the bridge which became fast on the rocks on the shore of the Redmond farm is still there.*

So what was to be done with the section that washed up against the Essex Junction dam? The *Burlington Daily News* kept its readers well informed.

*"Remove Bridge From Essex Dam: Men in Boats Are Tearing Wreckage Apart to Prevent Damage Being Done"*

*The water in the Winooski river in the vicinity of the large dam at the power plant of the Burlington Light and Power company at Essex Junction, is reported as receding steadily. The measurement taken last night showed 3.9 feet flowing over the dam, while this morning the water had dropped to an even three feet, and is still going down.*

*The amount of water steadily decreasing made the chances of the portion of Williston bridge going over the dam very slight. Rather than have the wreckage in the stream continually washed against the dam, the effect of which might weaken the structure to a certain extent it was deemed advisable to clear the timbers from the river. The work of removing the debris was commenced this morning. The task is not exceedingly dangerous as the wreckage is on the Williston side of the river, and out of the swift current. Men in boats are doing the work. The only danger connected with the work is the possibility of slipping into the icy waters. It is not expected that the work will take a long time.*

The section that lodged on the Redmond property caused a dispute between Rob Redmond and the town of Williston. The selectboard was a little too slow in reestablishing ownership of this part of the bridge. Rob Redmond claimed that, after thirty days, the bridge was abandoned property. The town brought legal action but lost in court. Reportedly, the lumber from the bridge became a barn.

Tarrier tells the story differently. He says the timbers were used to build a house for his uncle, the hired man on the farm.

It is hard to imagine, but apparently some did not want to replace the bridge. The *Burlington Free Press* lent its editorial support to construction of a new bridge stating:

*The loss of the bridge means isolation or a long detour via Essex Junction or the overpass a little this side of Richmond and another bridge in close conjunction. One of the questions asked of us at the Chittenden county road conference was, "Will the Williston bridge be replaced?" The query startled us. We had not supposed any other course than reconstruction and had even suggested itself. No bridge over the Winooski between Essex Junction and a point near Richmond is a situation which is unthinkable. It is to be hoped that all concerned may take prompt steps to bring about the replacing of the lost bridge with a new structure raised high enough so that even a repetition of the unusual conditions which prevailed this spring for the first time in sixty years or so will not suffice to sweep it from its foundations.*

## Replacing the Covered Bridge

Again, legal considerations entered the picture when the towns of Essex and Williston were faced with the costs of replacing the covered bridge. There was disagreement between the towns on who would pay how much. Essex and Williston sought relief in Chittenden County Court from paying the full cost. They made a case for the benefits accorded to other towns, such as Jericho, Underhill and Richmond by a North Williston bridge. But unlike the covered bridge, for which the cost was borne by surrounding towns, it was Essex, Williston and the state that ended up paying for the new bridge.

A court-ordered commission sided with the towns against the state and determined that the "petitioning towns would each be excessively burdened" by the expense. The report of the commissioners for the March 1924 term ordered the state to pay up to one-half of the cost, $51,575, of a new bridge, with 29 percent from Williston and 21 percent from Essex.

A historical assessment done in 1991 by Sivanuja S. Sundaram of the Vermont Agency of Transportation traced the history of the replacement bridge. The 289-foot-long, 19-foot-wide bridge was constructed in 1925 by the Standard Engineering and Contracting Company of Toledo, Ohio. In 1991, it was the only known surviving bridge in Vermont built by this company. It was one of the few Pennsylvania trusses in Vermont made of single-span steel. The concrete slab deck was placed on steel grating. The abutments were made of poured concrete.

## No Bridge Again

In the 1980s, several measures were taken to extend the life of the bridge and limit the wear and tear of the traffic. In 1984, the bridge's weight limit became posted as twelve tons "due to structural inadequacy." Grooves were

The dismantling of the steel bridge in preparation for its replacement. *Courtesy of Gisele Fontaine.*

The steel bridge sits in the Winooski River. *Courtesy of Gisele Fontaine.*

cut on the bridge deck to deal with expansion and contraction problems in 1988. In 1989, traffic was limited to one-way with a stop sign at each end, and the bridge was posted for three tons.

The bridge experienced several short-term closures. A May 24, 1985 *Essex Reporter* article, "Don't Be Stupid and Drive Over Bridge," warns drivers of the work slated for "removal of five sections of decking and cutting out the beams that hold them." Dennis Lutz, Essex Town Public Works superintendent, hoped to have the work done in two weeks.

On September 29, 1989, the *Free Press* reported the bridge was closed again due to a buckled deck. Nearby resident Michael Fontaine lamented the loss of traffic and customers for his pumpkin stand. At the same time, his father, Raymond Fontaine, said, "It was so peaceful and quiet here this morning I could hardly sleep."

Commuters could see a permanent closing of the bridge was in sight, and finally, on May 16, 1990, the bridge was closed to all traffic.

For the next two years and two months, North Williston became quieter and more isolated. Traffic was diverted to the crossings in Richmond and Essex Junction. North Williston resident Stephen Mease states, "Our kids were young. It was a time when you could walk down the street and visit friends without fearing for your life."

A recurring problem in the North Williston bridge area was the localized flooding on the Essex side whenever a thaw brought up the river level and ice blocked the flow. So the plans for the third bridge included reconstruction of 2,100 feet of North Williston Road in Essex, north of the bridge. Documentation of the historic nature of the steel bridge delayed the construction process.

The *Essex Reporter* noted the new bridge opened to traffic in June 1993 under budget and four months ahead of schedule.

Flooding still occurs occasionally on the Essex side, and commuters can be faced with a longer drive when the road is closed.

The controversial nature of the North Williston bridges has continued. Essex and Williston disagree on the appropriate weight limit for the bridge. On the Williston side, the road and bridge are posted for twenty-four thousand pounds, mainly a reflection of the residential nature of North Williston and the wishes of the residents to avoid becoming a major truck route.

On the Essex side, it is a different story. The North Williston Road in Essex is also posted for twenty-four thousand pounds, but Essex will issue permits so that truckers can exceed the limit if they wish. The Town of Williston will not issue permits for truckers to exceed the weight limit.

Construction company owner Gary Grzywna of Richmond objected to the double standard. The longer drive to his various construction jobs was a drain on his time and fuel budget.

"We might not look like a neighborhood, but it definitely is," according to North Williston resident Marianne Riordan, quoted in the *Free Press* on August 13, 2007. She was strongly in favor of the Williston selectboard maintaining the weight limit.

So, from 1860 to the present day, with the exception of a few years in the 1920s and early 1990s, North Williston has been connected to northern towns with a bridge across the Winooski River, with the steel bridge so far holding the record for longevity.

## *Chapter 7*

# The General Store

## *"A Community Gathering Place"*

The history of country stores is deeply intertwined with life in Vermont. Where there were roads, there came stores. Farmers, stores. Railroads, stores. Local needs, stores. Tourists, stores. It is a village culture, and villages ultimately give life to these stores," states Dennis Bathory-Kitz in *A History and Guide: Country Stores of Vermont*.

No other institution in North Williston was the center of this vibrant community more than Roswell E. Brown's store. With the post office and the telephone exchange inside, the store functioned as the heart of the village, officially and socially. The store was located on land now occupied by 2523 North Williston Road at the intersection with Chapman Lane.

Frederick Simonds established the first North Williston general store in a railroad building in 1865. The post office, with Simonds as the postmaster, started at the same time. In 1873, Jonathan R. Talcott took over the duties of storekeeper and postmaster, followed by John Whitcomb in 1879.

Brown had the longest tenure as the North Williston storekeeper, from 1894 to about 1933, and is the name that is most closely associated with the store. Brown was the youngest son of Reed and Electa Brown, born on November 4, 1853, in Fletcher, Vermont. He was educated in Williston, Richmond and Essex. He manufactured butter tubs for about ten years with his father but spent most of his working life as the storekeeper in North Williston.

Julia (Mentzer) Fifield remembers him as "a sprightly man, small in stature, soft spoken, and very much a business man. He had little time for idle chatter…He served his customers with 'the patience of Job,' especially children… [He] was truly a busy business man."

Roswell E. Brown photo from the 1898 Legislative Souvenir. *Courtesy of University of Vermont Special Collections.*

Brown represented Williston as a Republican in the state legislature in 1898. He married Julia Martin of Corona, Michigan, on September 4, 1879. They had three children: Arthur E., born in 1883; A. Carlyle, born in 1884; and Charles M., born in1889.

Folklorist Jane C. Beck writes, "In Vermont the general store linked farmers together and more often than not provided the impetus for the growth of the community."

North Williston resident and farmer Bob Chapman certainly agrees: "There's one thing that's interesting about that store. It wasn't just the store; it was a community gathering place. And when all the farmers went to the creamery in the morning, they didn't go right home. They went to the store and they sat around there and they gabbed, and that yard was just full of horses."

One of the Chapman's horses, in particular, took advantage of the daily gatherings in front of Brown's store. "We had an old horse named Pete to take the milk [to the creamery] and [my father would] leave him out there, and old Pete wised up, and if somebody put a loaf of bread in the back of his wagon, old Pete would go get it. That wasn't too bad, because a loaf of bread was eight cents and [you could buy] five gallons of gas for a dollar."

It was up to Bob Chapman's father, Lucian Paul Chapman, to replace the purloined loaves. "And my father bought more loaves of bread."

Fifield describes the horse and wagon traffic this way: "The Brown's customers came from miles around. The store provided tie-ups for teams while their drivers were shopping. Often there were many teams crowding the front of the building. On the back lot there was a long free-standing shed closed on three sides with tie-ups for visiting teams used when a daylong train trip was necessary. That was a parking garage a la 1900!"

A June 1917 railroad right-of-way map, indeed, shows an outline of the shed, as well as an area marked "stock yards."

Fifield recalls the exterior of the store:

> *On the end near the railroad were steps. On the opposite end was an outside stairway for the second floor apartment. A bit off the building's center was*

Notice the building in back of the store, which was used for teams as the owners took the train somewhere for the day. *Courtesy of Gertrude Gonyo.*

> *a wide heavy door, the entrance to the store. This door was double in width and opened with an iron thumb latch, a challenge for small hands. This door was flanked by two large windows for light, not for show. The main entrance steps, in line with the wide door, were built into the porch to keep them free of snow and rain. There was a normal door to the left of the store entrance. This led to the office and to the switchboard for Brown's Telephone Line. This small room had space for the modest switchboard and the one and only operator. A door to the store gave Mr. Brown the opportunity to supervise if necessary.*

Socializing also took place inside the store. Fifield remembers the interior:

> *A large potbellied stove [was] surrounded by hard-bottomed chairs, some stools, and often an upturned nail keg. The overall number of seats was determined by the season of the year. In fall and winter, the area could be well populated. I often lingered by the stove, that is, until my mother discovered me there. She thought (and I am sure she was correct) that the language, the gossip, and the stories told were not for young ears. For me, the laughter was the fascination. The…building was far from luxurious. It was totally utilitarian. A covered porch six or eight feet in width ran the length of the street side.*

On May 7, 1898, the *Burlington Clipper* reported that "R.E. Brown is building a large piazza on his store."

Bathory-Kitz claims, "Vermonters never loved their country stores, never recount store stories. Churches and meetinghouses and inns and houses are local characters, but save for David Budbill's *Judevine*, Walter Hard's *A Mountain Township* or Nancy Tschorn's *Country Store Stories*, the lowly store escapes memory."

This was not the case in North Williston. Fifield remembers the store as her "home away from home."

> [It] *was a wonderful place and I always used to wait around all the time for the drummers to come. The drummer…was the man that came around with a horse and wagon and laid out all the clothes on the counters. I used to go up and have a great time because I would once in a while be able to buy a sweater or something. I was always very athletic in my early days and I always liked those men's sweaters, the heavy ones that had just the square neck, and I could always get one from the drummer.*

> *Mr. Brown always invited my mother to come when the dry goods drummer was at the store to help select the items. In return for her help, she often bought boots and sweaters for me at a lower price. I longed to be with her just to look and sometimes I was invited.*

The drummer was the connection between a wholesale distributor and a storekeeper. He arrived with catalogs and samples in trunks trying to drum up business.

Walter A. Friedman, in *Birth of a Salesman: The Transformation of Selling in America*, writes, "[D]rummers sold the goods that stocked the general stores found at country crossroads. Such stores carried a tremendous range of items, including fruit and candy, nails and hinges, horse collars, lamps, cloth, wire, netting, cord, alcohol, paint and leather goods."

Fifield remembers the wide variety of food and items available at Brown's store:

> *Women's clothes, women's underwear, buttons, threads, needles, salt fish… horse collars, horse liniment…dry goods. Everything that you needed, he had…* [Y]*ou bought saltine crackers from those things with the glass front and a tin cover…and pickles out of a barrel. And salt fish, salt salmon, salt cod all out of a barrel. You provided your own platter for the fish…* [M]*olasses with a pump. You would take a bottle up and they would pump it out…if it wasn't too cold.*

A November 1909 calendar advertises that R.E. Brown & Co. are "dealers in groceries, boots, shoes, dry goods, fur coats, and all kinds of general merchandise, flour, feed, salt, wagons, open and top buggies, harnesses, and farm implements."

Bob Chapman would get ready for fishing by shopping at the store: "Every spring I could buy a new fish pole. They had fish poles there about thirty feet long. Bamboo pole, a quarter a piece, and then you could buy a fish line, a green string wrapped on a reel. And it had a hook and a sinker on it too, for ten cents. And I could get a new fish pole, a line, and a straw hat every spring."

The Wright family contributed to the economy of Williston and beyond, through purchases for their businesses and home. Smith Wright and his sons patronized John Whitcomb when he was the North Williston storekeeper and later Brown. They also shopped at the Charles Warren store in the village of Williston.

North Williston, Vt.,..................189

M C J & C S Wright

BOUGHT OF

R. E. BROWN,
GENERAL MERCHANDISE

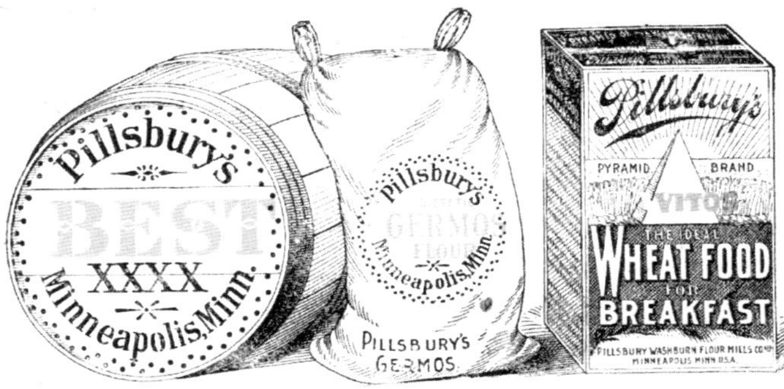


| | | | |
|---|---|---|---|
| Nov 2 | To 10 Glass | | 40 |
| " 4 | " 1 " | | 8 |
| " 6 | " 3 " | | 24 |
| " " | " 1# Putty | | 4 |
| " " | " 5 gal K Oil | | 60 |

BE NOT DECEIVED "PILLSBURY'S BEST" IS THE BEST
Insist upon having this World Renowned Flour, and no other

An R.E. Brown invoice. *Courtesy of James and Lucille McCullough.*

The receipts in the Smith Wright papers show that Clinton and Clayton Wright purchased a variety of items at Brown's store: nails, paint, pails, putty, an alarm clock, oyster shells, sperm oil, cigars, bran for animal feed, mouse traps, shredded biscuits, German syrup (a patent medicine), pipe tobacco, matches, cheese, chimneys for lamps, rope, hinges, eggs, mittens, axle grease, a potato hook, lard, broom, Gold Dust (washing powder), soda and lemons. The wide selection of goods and products made this truly a general store.

The receipts indicate the shopping was done piecemeal, buying one or two items per day over the course of a month. The Wright brothers would run up a bill and deal with it at the end of the month. Most tabs totaled less than fifty dollars, and many less than ten dollars.

Lucia (Chapman) Willard, Bob Chapman's sister, recounts her favorite story about the store and how she devised a plan to get her hands on some of the special cookies she craved:

> *They had cookies in boxes with a glass front, and they had these wonderful, wonderful cookies with pink tops with coconut, and I used to stand in front of those boxes. I wanted one of those pink and white cookies. And my mother would say "No, no, you cannot have those, they are too expensive. They are not good for you." And I could never have those nice little cookies with the pink frosting and white coconut.*
>
> *I was always trying to figure out how to get some of those cookies. Of course you could go up to the store and charge things, you didn't have to pay for them. They would write it down and send it home once a month. So my mother's birthday was coming up, I kept wondering what was I going to get her…then it dawned on me. I stopped at the store on the way home from school, and I said, "I want a bag of those cookies. I want some pink ones and I want some white ones." So George Irish said okay. So he bagged up the cookies for me. I went home and I could not get home fast enough. I came bounding in the house and I said "Oh, mama, I got your birthday present. I got your birthday present." And she opened up the bag and all she could do was stand there and laugh.*

While Lucia Willard had an honest approach to getting her favorite cookies, Beck tells us that shoplifting could be a problem in country stores. She says thievery was dealt with in a quiet fashion without a big scene, probably due to the storekeeper knowing just about everybody who came in. Sometimes storekeepers just put the cost of the stolen items on the running tab.

The North Williston store was not immune to theft, as this 1916 newspaper item notes: "After they had cut a network of wires leading into the telephone exchange, which is located in the store of R.E. Brown, of North Williston, burglars entered the store during the early morning hours and got away with $150 in cash, which they took from the safe, and a watch valued at $10. The robbery occurred on November 10."

Besides all the items the store carried, Brown's would be called upon to handle orders for special occasions. On July 31, 1913, Williston celebrated the 150th anniversary of its 1763 charter. The events included a parade; races; dinner at thirty-five cents a plate; a baseball game between Essex and Richmond; music from Sherman's Military Band from Burlington; orations, including one by the governor; a historical poem by Daniel L. Cady; a school reunion; an evening program depicting historical episodes from Williston's past; and fireworks.

A receipt in the Williston Historical Society collection shows that Brown, who served on the general anniversary organizing committee, handled the finances for the baseball game. He collected $54.75 in ticket sales, and the expenses consisted of paying the teams $28.00, buying three baseballs for $3.75 and three straps for $1.20. This left a balance on hand of $21.80.

Brown's store served as a local purchasing agent for several Williston town projects. Some of the items for the 1923 upgrade of the North Williston school were purchased through the store. The 1918 town report mentions six hundred cement bags and twenty-five cedar posts, apparently for bridge construction. If Brown didn't have something in stock, he could get it for his customers.

In earlier days, Brown's store hosted other social functions. An article by Myrtle Lane in the June–August 1976 *Chittenden County Historical Society Bulletin* states, "The building had multiple uses besides selling merchandise and being the post office. Mrs. Linda Tarrier, who has lived in Williston over eighty years, remembers dances and theatricals held upstairs. Traveling companies would perform, hiring local people for small parts; she and her sister played some bit roles."

On February 8, 1912, the *Bristol (VT) Herald* (as quoted in *Richmond, Vermont: A History of More than 200 Years*) reported that: "About 18 couples from here [Richmond] attended the poverty party at Brown's Hall, North Williston, Friday night, going on the mail train which was over an hour late, and returning on the midnight express which was also late so the party did not reach home until four o'clock in the morning. Barring the annoyance of waiting for trains, an enjoyable evening was spent."

A poverty party was a gathering with a theme: attendees' dress had to mimic poverty, prizes were common items, the invitations were often written in broken English and fines were levied for any clothing item contrary to the theme. Refreshments were simple and unadorned. Often the intent was to collect money and items for the less fortunate.

## The Telephone Exchange

Brown's store also housed the telephone exchange. The Vermont Public Service Commission reported the North Williston Telephone Company commenced on January 1, 1905, as a partnership between R.E. Brown and E.A. Brown. (This is probably a misprinted reference to Roswell Brown's oldest son Arthur Eugene.) The company served Williston, Essex, Shelburne, St. George and part of Richmond. In 1916, its net income was $211.60, and in 1917, it was $426.89.

According to Fifield:

> *For most of the people of Williston, Brown's line was their only phone service. A few had the added luxury of New England Telephone and Telegraph. When the operator of Brown's line was not on duty, calls were limited to one's own line only by cranking the person's ring on one's own phone line. It was truly a rural system. "Listening in" was the pastime of some. This system did connect to the outside, but only in the daytime hours when the operator was on duty.*

One great attraction for Fifield was the chance to play phone operator: "I use to stay there hour after hour and plug in the plugs for [the operator]. [She would] give us lollipops. I used to love that store, but of course I liked the telephone part the best. I had such fun in there; I got everyone's lines mixed up…You could listen to what everyone said."

Fifield's telephone mischief extended beyond the confines of Brown's store and North Williston to the Wright house on Governor Chittenden Road: "They had a New England line and Brown's line in one room at their house. We were bad children and if we ever found them ringing at the same time, we would take the receivers and switch them."

## THE POST OFFICE

Since the post office was located in the North Williston store, the storekeeper and postmaster were often one and the same person, but at times, the positions were held by two different people.

Author Beck recounts the duties of the postmaster: "Sorted mail, sold stamps, coped with packages…six days a week." This brought in extra income and solidified the store as a community center.

According to Fifield, Brown sorted the North Williston personal mail and placed it in the mailboxes for pickup; it was not delivered to the houses. A mail car was standard on all passenger trains. Mail was sorted on the train and bagged for the various stops on the line. Outgoing mail bags could be snatched from a post near the station, and incoming bags were dropped.

The mail was taken to the post office in the village of Williston by the stage that ran several times a day.

The North Williston post office moved to the Pratt homestead near the bridge (now 2738 North Williston Road) in 1942 "because of a squabble over a registered letter." Lillian Pratt, the daughter of John Pratt, was the postmistress until the office closed in 1944. It had been in operation since 1865.

The store building as an apartment house, circa 1972. *Courtesy of the Chittenden County Historical Society and the University of Vermont Special Collections.*

"Storekeepers were often ground down by work, poor finances and unpaid customer credit. As they grew older, their stores grew as shopworn as they themselves," writes Bathory-Kitz.

Roswell E. Brown died on September 15, 1937, at age eighty-three, but he had suffered a stroke at about age eighty, so it is possible that George F. Irish had taken over the store sometime earlier than when it was officially sold to him on February 16, 1938. Irish had been a clerk at the store since age fourteen, going back to 1881.

Mr. and Mrs. Sidney E. Greenwood, George Irish's daughter and son-in-law, were the next proprietors, starting in 1943. Joseph King took over from the Greenwoods, and it closed soon thereafter. The building was changed to apartments.

Raymond Fontaine states his brother-in-law, Arthur Yandow, bought some of the contents of the store—the clock and display cases—when it went out of business.

In 1973, a Chittenden County Historical Society publication, *Look Around Essex and Williston, Vermont*, lamented the disappearance of many of the buildings in the once-bustling community of North Williston, except "the old store building, now in seeming unending makeover into apartments."

The former store building was destroyed when a "spectacular fire" broke out April 11, 1985, but the Geraw family, living there at the time, only escaped with minor injuries.

Fifield sums up the role of the store this way: "Brown's store was the corner store of the village. News and problems were aired, shared, and often solved within the store's four walls. It was a Mecca for young and old and all in between."

## The Song: "Rozie Brown's Store"

In 1990, Vermont singer/songwriter Margaret MacArthur was an artist in residence at Williston Central School in preparation of the upcoming celebration of Vermont's bicentennial in 1991. She wrote several songs with the students, and "Rozie Brown's Store" covered some aspects of North Williston history. It was included in the *Vermont Heritage Songbook*, recorded in 1994 and reproduced here by permission.

*"Rozie Brown's Store"*
*By Margaret MacArthur*

*CHORUS*
*First came the railroad*
*Then came the depot*
*Then came the general store,*
*Gathering place for the people*

*Rozie Brown's store had everything and more*
*That anybody could need*
*Fishing pole, hook line and sinker*
*Pins and needles and thread*
*Horse collars, straw hats and clothes*
*Barrels of pickles and fish*
*Cookies and crackers, pump your own molasses*
*You can get anything you wish*

*CHORUS*

*The farmer's big hands would roll the milk cans*
*Onto the train to Boston*
*Then drive their teams back to the store*
*For gabbin' and for talkin'*
*Telephone exchange didn't cost any change*
*We could help plug in the wire*
*Sort the mail, put it in a big bag*
*Hook it to the fast train "Flyer"*

*CHORUS*

*First freezing plant in all this land*
*Was by the store and the railroad track*
*When the cove was frozen men would go out knowin'*
*Time to cut the Chapman Cove ice*
*From here you could see all the geese who would flee*
*'Til all the hill looked white*
*A boy drove geese to the freezing plant*
*A boy in command all right*

*CHORUS*

*We saw the bridge go down by ice coming up*
*In nineteen twenty three*
*It floated on down the Winooski River*
*Pushed by a big elem tree.*
*To slide down Depot Hill was a great big thrill*
*All the way to the railroad track*
*After a chill or a winter spill*
*We'd go to Rozie Brown's before headin' back.*

*CHORUS*
*Repeat first stanza.*

*Chapter 8*

# The Dairy Industry in North Williston

The nature of Vermont agriculture in the late 1800s transitioned from sheep to dairy products: cheese and butter and eventually fluid milk. Several dairy-based businesses had their headquarters in North Williston and took advantage of shipping by rail. Unlike the general store in North Williston, the line of ownership for many of these businesses is marked by transfers, partnerships, dissolution and disappearances from the historic record.

E.R. Crane and David Brown built a cheese factory in 1868 as one of the earliest industries in North Williston. It was owned by several people over the years. In 1869, Crane bought out Brown for $2,250. A year later, Crane sold the business to T.E. and L.E. Dunlap of Westford for $7,000. Smith Wright bought the business in 1885. The transfer to Smith Wright, as noted in Williston land records, included "all the machinery and tools now on the premises that are used for the manufacture of Butter and cheese. Also all the logs that convey the whey to the tanks, and the tanks themselves."

Smith Wright's involvement in the cheese-making business is well documented in his records. For example, on page 580 of his account book for 1872–1883, he lists the people who received dividends from the North Williston Cheese Company on June 22, 1878. The prominent Williston names include several Whitcombs, Fays and Metcalfs. George Chapman and Smith Wright are also included, and L.E. Dunlap earned $140.62 for making the cheese. Historian J. Kevin Graffagnino states that the cheese plant shut down in the late 1890s.

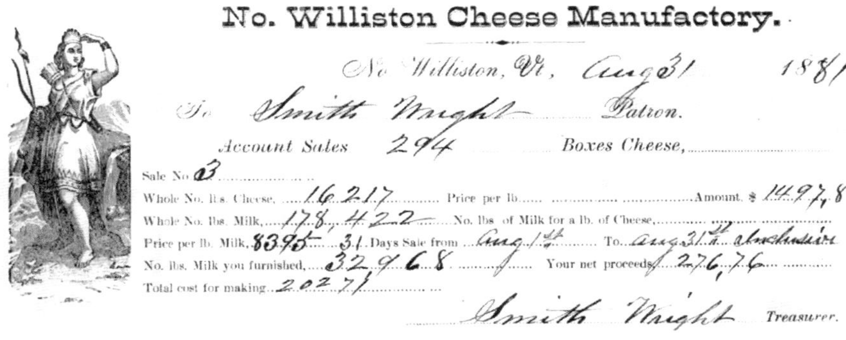

No. Williston Cheese Manufactory.

No. Williston, Vt., Aug 31 1881

To Smith Wright Patron.

Account Sales 294 Boxes Cheese,

Sale No 3

Whole No. lbs. Cheese, 16217 Price per lb. Amount, $ 1497,86

Whole No. lbs. Milk, 178,422 No. lbs of Milk for a lb. of Cheese,

Price per lb. Milk, 8395 31 Days Sale from Aug 1st To Aug 31st inclusive

No. lbs. Milk you furnished, 32968 Your net proceeds 276,76

Total cost for making 20271

Smith Wright Treasurer.

A record of an 1881 Smith Wright transaction at the North Williston Cheese Manufactory. *Courtesy of James and Lucille McCullough.*

## CREAMERIES

The Winooski Valley Co-operative Creamery was organized March 13, 1899, for the purpose of "manufacturing and selling dairy products." The principal owners, as recorded on March 13, 1899, in the Vermont Records of Inactive Corporations, were E.C. Fay, president; M.W. Chapman; H.M. Fay, secretary; John Whitcomb; and I.B. Whitcomb. The building was located north of the tracks.

Around 1905, the Winooski Valley Co-operative Creamery became known as the Winooski Valley Creamery Company and was dissolved on February 12, 1912. On this same date, the building and equipment were sold to Clayton J. Wright, son of Smith Wright, and James E. Kennedy. In 1913, Wright and Kennedy leased the operation to H.P. Hood and Son. Wright sold out to Kennedy in 1919. Hood operated the plant until 1937.

According to historian Gerald Fox, the term creamery could refer to many different types of dairy operations.

> *When the word "creamery" was first coined, it referred to any building where butter was made. With the introduction of the centrifugal cream separator, the industrial cream processing industry adopted the word to mean a building where that process was in use. However, as the dairy business changed over to fluid milk, the direct connection to butter was lost. By the 1930s a creamery could be anything from a milk gathering station to a bottling plant to a dairy processing company.*

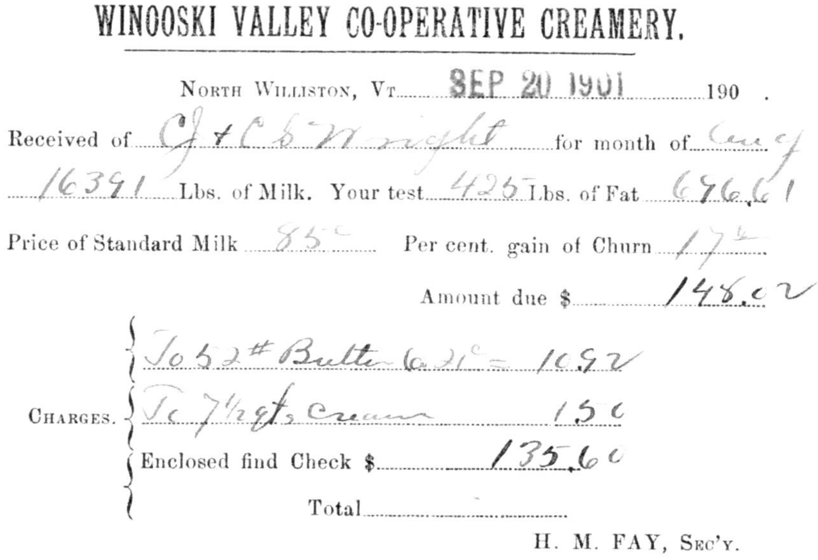

WINOOSKI VALLEY CO-OPERATIVE CREAMERY.

North Williston, Vt. SEP 20 1901 190 .

Received of C J & C S Wright for month of Aug

16391 Lbs. of Milk. Your test 4.25 Lbs. of Fat 696.61

Price of Standard Milk 85c Per cent. gain of Churn 17

Amount due $ 148.02

Charges. To 52# Butter @ 21c = 10.92

To 7½ qts Cream 1.50

Enclosed find Check $ 135.60

Total

H. M. FAY, Sec'y.

A 1901 Winooski Valley Co-operative Creamery receipt for Clinton and Clayton Wright for a delivery of milk. *Courtesy of James and Lucille McCullough.*

The Hood Company also built a milk platform on the south side of the tracks in 1913 and, in 1917, a milk storage or processing plant. An icehouse was added in 1922. Here, milk cans were stored on ice and loaded onto trains.

Hood shut down this building in 1937 and transferred ownership to the Richmond Co-op on December 12, 1938. In 1951, the co-op sold the building to Fred Shattuck and Norm Burnett, who tore it down.

## Milk Cans

Farmers often used unique methods when they shipped milk from the farm to the creamery. Oscar Cooley, in *When Grandpa was a Boy*, remembers how a piece of sterile cheesecloth was placed over the mouth of the milk can before the milk was poured in. Before the cans were hauled to the milk plant, "a thick, felt cover, shaped to fit the can," was put in place to keep the milk cool on its way.

Harold F. Wilson, in *The Hill Country of Northern New England*, quotes a 1905 U.S. Department of Agriculture report that milk cans could also be "covered with a horse blanket or piece of canvas. When the distance was long, a cake of ice often had to be placed under the cover in summer or a lighted lantern in winter."

William James of Middlebury wrote to the *Burlington Free Press* in 1982 with this remembrance:

> *I lived in North Williston about 1917 or '18 until 1920. I was about 8, 9, and 10 years old at the time and my father managed the milk plant for H.P. Hood and Sons…At that time they would fill a large ice house with cakes of ice cut on the Chapman pond to cool the milk. The ice house was attached to the milk plant. We had to put these cans of milk into large vats and cover them with ice. When it was about time for the train, we had to pull these cans of milk out of the vats and all hands rolled the cans onto the train. (Those days even young boys had work to do.) It was pretty rough when they were initiating a new man on the train.*

Bob Chapman vividly remembers how milk was shipped out of North Williston several years after William James's time. He describes how the milk plant was equipped with a holding tank for cooling the milk.

> *The teams used to all come down with their milk and they dumped the milk in and they cooled it and then they would put it back in the cans… Every day there was a milk train came along that went through to Boston and they'd pull up to the door and stop and put out a gangplank and they'd start rolling these milk cans. Boy! They were good at it. These guys, they could roll those and they could go ten feet before another guy would catch it just on its edge…*

Gertrude Gonyo was bothered by the noise of the milk cans: "Some of my earliest memories was sleeping out on the front porch on the main road in the house [at 2454 North Williston Road]…and hearing the clatter of those dog-gone milk cans because in the summer I liked to sleep outside and I never slept very late, I can tell you, because of those milk cans."

Small milk cans could hold eight and a half quarts and be fairly easy to handle. But larger milk cans held ten gallons or eighty-six pounds of milk. The cans weighed twenty-five to thirty pounds; whether they were full or empty, it took impressive strength to move them. Cans remained buoyant in a vat filled with ice and water, but once out of the vat, they were very heavy. Some milk facilities employed a hoist system, whether on the farm, at the

"Milk Maid with Cans." Blanche Bailey Chapman, wife of Lucian Paul Chapman, shows one of the duties of a farmer's wife, circa 1927. *Courtesy of Connie Chapman Dumas.*

railroad siding or at the creamery. The cans were numbered so they could be returned to their proper owners.

According to Jan Albers, in *Hands on the Land, A History of the Vermont Landscape*, the transition from milk cans to bulk tanks was a major expense for small farms and signaled "a revolution" in dairy farming: "A bulk tank is a large stainless steel cooling tank capable of holding all the milk a farm can produce in a couple of days. In addition to the considerable expense of the tank itself, it required its own "milk house," a room connected to the barn, with a cement floor and electricity to run its cooling system. A large tanker truck would then suck the milk out of the tank with a hose and haul it to the creamery."

Other Williston residents benefited from the milk plant in North Williston. Suppers at the Federated church were a challenge without hot water. A 1981 *Vermont Life* article, "Williston's Chicken Pie Suppers," by George Bellerose recounts: "'Until 1951 when we got water at the church, the boys would have to bring hot water in milk cans from the North Williston Creamery for drinking and some washing,' Ada Talcott recalls. 'And in those days, we didn't have church dishes and each hostess would have to find enough dishes for three sittings, lug them in, and then take them home dirty the next morning and clean them.'"

The H.P. Hood milk storage building is on the far left, and the depot is in the center of this photo. *Courtesy of Williston Historical Society.*

The foundation of the milk storage building south of the tracks still remains. *Courtesy of the author.*

## The Browns' Butter Tubs

The butter tub manufactory of Reed Brown and his son, Roswell, was another early dairy-based industry in North Williston. The business, which was established by Wilkins & Loggins in 1872, was taken over by the Browns around 1874. Eight years later, they employed ten men and produced $12,000 worth of butter tubs per year.

Reed Brown's two other sons were also connected to an industry in North Williston. According to a 1933 obituary for Bertrand F. Brown, Bertrand and his brother, Byron B., were involved in a box manufacturing firm in North Williston. It is not clear if this was one and the same as the butter tub factory.

Smith Wright, frequent customer of the Browns' business, bought 144 butter tubs from them for $30.24, at a cost of $0.21 each, on February 7, 1880. Butter tubs in Vermont and northern New York were generally made of spruce and came in twenty-, forty- and sixty-pound increments for large shipments. Smaller tubs could contain two, three or even five pounds of butter.

The rail facilities in North Williston served the area farmers well from the 1860s to the 1950s with a cheese factory, a butter tub producer and several creameries.

## *Chapter 9*

# The Schools

## *From "Unfit" to "Superior"*

The history of the North Williston School District can be traced back to 1840, when the North Williston area split from the much larger original District 2 that had been established in 1795. The first North Williston school was located on the west side of North Williston Road between Fay Lane and the railroad tracks. According to Carol Dean, in *The History of Schools in Williston, Vermont*, this school was in sad shape in the early 1860s. The building measured eleven by twenty feet, without a convenient woodshed, no fence around the playground and only eight square feet of blackboard. During the 1863–1864 school year, thirteen families sent twenty-one children to the school that was termed "unfit" and valued at $0.

The second school, which still stands today, cost $950 at the time of its construction in 1864. One claim to fame for this school is that it became the first one in Williston to earn a "Superior School" rating from the state. The town report for the year ending February 6, 1923, proudly states that the North Williston school received a score of ninety-three out of one hundred on the state rating card for rural schools: "Lighting, heating and ventilation, toilets, blackboards, text books, drinking arrangements, flag, training and experience, efficiency, professional spirit and living conditions of the teacher are points which must be right in order to receive credit for standardization. The State aids $500 in establishing these schools."

The 1923 town report also details the purchase of chair desks, chemical toilets, a heater, maps and globe, wiring and electrical fixtures and books for the school library. Storekeeper R.E. Brown received payment for a clock, doormats and poles for the swings. John R. Forville got $675 for

The front of the second North Williston School in the early days. *Courtesy of Williston Historical Society.*

remodeling the building. All told, $1,453 was spent to bring the school its superior rating.

"We cordially invite the taxpayers to visit the North Williston school and inspect the building and equipment. We feel sure that all will then join with the School Directors in expressing gratitude to the Selectmen for their part in accomplishing this good work," invited the school directors in the town report.

Lucia (Chapman) Willard attended the school in the 1920s and recounted to Dean how the girls would put together decorated box lunches that were auctioned off to the boys. The money raised was used to buy school supplies. The railroad repair crews called in after the 1927 flood also gladly participated in the box lunch auctions. Willard remembers the wood room and two bathrooms as part of the structure and the classroom with an organ.

Gertrude Gonyo remembers another school lunch tradition: "I can remember that all the neighbors in North Williston got together, and each one that had children in school would each have their day when they would bring in a hot casserole, so we had hot lunches at noon…Maybe it would be once a week, that it would be my mother's turn to make a casserole dish to furnish the hot lunch for everybody."

From the school registers, Dean notes several special occasions at the school. A 1922 Halloween social raised $10 to help with the purchase of a Victrola. On a 1935 field trip to Burlington, the students toured the airport, the Fleming Museum and the fire station. There was manual training for the boys where they made "door stops, bows and arrows…large kites."

Margaret "Peg" Chapman taught all eight grades at the North Williston school from 1937 to 1940. The eighth graders would move up to the Village School after the year began. The school day went from 9:00 a.m. to 4:00 p.m. for twenty-five to thirty students, ages five to fifteen.

Chapman used a curriculum from the state to keep the subjects and grade levels separate. She supplemented her lessons with newspapers and magazines. As for books, she picked them up from the town library or had the children bring their own.

There was a baby grand piano in the school. Chapman would lay out the books and lessons for each group to keep things organized. She needed good lesson plans to get through the day. She was not sick very often and didn't recall having a substitute. There was no phone in the school.

Art was limited to Friday afternoons. Health consisted of a checklist for each student on personal hygiene: brushing teeth, cleaning fingernails, etc. The outdoors was used for science: nature study and a wildflower contest. Some boys brought in snakes, and she would tell the students that the first graders were terrified of them, so the snakes had to go. But, actually, it was Chapman who disliked the snakes.

Recess games would include a ball, swings and snow games. The children liked to visit with friends who they wouldn't have a chance to see after school, especially those from another part of town, such as Mountain View Road. Students from that section of town came to school in a van or sedan.

She recalls that drinking water was kept in a porcelain jug with a spout. Children brought their own lunches, and there was a burner in the back of the room for soup or something hot from the parents.

Chapman earned eighteen dollars a week and was paid seven dollars for room and board. She was terrified of wood fires and fearful of the "monster of a stove" with all the firewood. She was grateful that one of the big boys built a fire in the morning.

The children did not have to deal with a cold walk in the winter to use the bathroom because it was located inside the front entrance on the left, and on the right, there was the woodshed.

They had Halloween and Christmas programs at the school. In fact, Chapman met her husband-to-be, Bob, after a Halloween party at the school. Bob Chapman's sister, Lucia, stayed to help clean up afterward. They had harvest vegetables as decorations. Bob Chapman picked up a cabbage and threw it to his sister. She did not catch it, and it broke a window. Now what? Bob decided he had to fix it, and he did the next morning.

Margaret Chapman recalls this school prank from the days of when the cold storage plant was still standing:

> *Two boys came to the frozen food locker building and found lots of eggs out back. They thought it would be a nice thing to bring them to the school kids. So they wrapped them up and brought them up to the school kids. They put them in each lunch box, which was kept out in the entry way. Stone cold, ice cold. Well the kind teacher said in the middle of the morning, "Maybe you kids should bring your lunch boxes into the classroom. They will be warm this noon." Frozen eggs did not stand the heat of the room. And the boys got their real comeuppance when* [it was] *decided there were only two lunch boxes without eggs.*

The closing of the school was a landmark event for North Williston. After the Village School burned down in 1949, Williston Central School opened in the fall of 1950 with eight classrooms and enough space to accommodate the entire first- through eighth-grade students in town. The outlying one-room schools were closed and, over the years, have met a series of fates: torn down, converted to residences and other uses.

Margaret Chapman and her class at North Williston School. *Courtesy of Connie Chapman Dumas.*

The North Williston school building in 1984 with the characteristic large windows. *Courtesy of the author.*

The school building in North Williston became a residence and is the only former public building in North Williston still remaining that was part of the busy times in that part of the town. As a residence at 62 Fay Lane, it has gone through many upgrades and additions, but the large windows that let in the daylight for the scholars are still there, reminding the careful observer of the role the building played in North Williston's history for eighty-six years.

## *Chapter 10*

# The Library Branch

The librarian's comments in the 1913 Williston town report stated that the North Williston Branch, with Mrs. Amy Warren, librarian, started on March 30, 1912, with a loan of fifty volumes. By December 14, 1912, forty-eight volumes had been exchanged.

The 1914 town report refers to North Williston as a branch library. In 1915, 150 volumes were loaned to the North Williston branch, and circulation was recorded at 200. The town report library notes continue to mention the North Williston library until 1917.

So where was this North Williston library located? The store would have been a logical place because it was centrally located with lots of traffic and open many hours. This situation would have been similar to that of the main Williston library. For many years, the main library was located on the second floor of Warren's store on the southeast corner of Williston Road and Oak Hill Road. Sylvia Warren served as the town librarian and postmistress, and, since the post office was located in the store, she could handle both jobs.

Mrs. Amy Warren, the North Williston librarian, lived in North Williston, so it is possible her house served as the library branch.

The town report library notes also tallied the number of books distributed to the one-room schools in town. In 1915, 320 volumes went out to nine schools. So perhaps the North Williston school served as a home for this branch of the library. But it should be noted that North Williston was listed separately as a branch of the library and not merely mentioned as one of the schools. That seems to indicate that it was located somewhere else.

The Sidney and Amy Warren house (now 2254 North Williston Road) that may have served as the North Williston branch of the Williston library, circa 1913 to 1917. *Courtesy of Williston Historical Society.*

Julia Fifield has this to say about a North Williston library:

> *While I lived in North Williston, I am sure there was no library building… Mrs. Amy Warren listed as librarian could be correct. My thinking is that she was a "go-between" librarian, borrowing a few books to have in her home and getting books on order from the Williston main library for North Williston residents. It could have been a service of the main library for North Williston residents with limited transportation, and there were many.*

Regardless of the exact location of the North Williston library branch, the notes in the town reports reflect the importance of North Williston as a vibrant part of the town. Several factors probably led to the decision to establish the branch: the demand for library services there, the difficulty of traveling to Williston to the main library located at that time in the Modern Woodmen of America building (now the Town Hall Annex) and the town's pride in providing library services to its citizens.

# Chapter 11
# Two Roads, Two Families

## Chapman Lane

Chapman Lane and Fay Lane, named for early families that settled in the area, are the two side roads in North Williston. They were, at one time, connected to roads to other parts of the town, as noted on several of the historic maps of Williston.

On September 25, 1867, the Williston Road Records, Volume 1, notes a petition signed by twenty citizens to the Williston selectboard to establish a road north of the railway from the depot to the residence of George A. Chapman. The petition was approved on October 12 by the selectmen, and Chapman Lane became a town highway.

Today, Chapman Lane generally follows the railroad tracks east to what was the Chapman farm. The Clark farm on Governor Chittenden Road, the original Thomas Chittenden homestead, was connected to Chapman Lane by a very rough road. A recently completed survey of ancient roads in Williston done by Ronald E. Gauthier concludes this was never a town road and was probably built only to accommodate farm traffic.

The condition of the road was recalled by former residents of North Williston. Charles Irish remembered riding his bike on this road over to Governor Chittenden Road, where it intersects Route 2 at the bottom of French Hill. There he hoped somebody would pick him up and give him a ride back to North Williston or at least to Williston. He said the road was "half way decent, far from their better ones."

Margaret Chapman recounts how Marvin Clark's father would take off his shoes to keep them clean as he walked along the road from the Clark farm to Chapman Lane on his way to school at the Classical Institute in Essex Center.

Julia Fifield states, "[W]hen I was little you could go from North Williston around to the [Thomas] Chittenden house. But only hang on with your teeth. It was almost a cow path. You could go on horseback, or you could go in a wagon, but very carefully even then."

Since the industries were located along Chapman Lane, it is noted as Mill Street on the 1915 Sanborn insurance map.

## Five Generations of the Chapman Family in North Williston

George A. Chapman came to Williston from Cavendish, Vermont, in 1840. Although, at times, George lived on the Jericho side of river, the North Williston farm was probably established in the early 1840s. Watrous and Betsey Thomson sold about 113 acres in Jericho to Chapman for $7,500 on April 24, 1860. This included about eighty acres "on the south side of Onion River" in Jericho and Williston, also known as Messenger's Island. In 1865, Chapman moved permanently to Williston. In the *Gazetteer and Business Directory of Chittenden County for 1882–1883*, Chapman and son are listed owning Durham cattle and a dairy with forty-five cows on 340 acres.

Marvin Wright Chapman was next in the Chapman line, followed by his son, Lucian Paul. Paul's son, Marvin B. "Bob," was the last Chapman to farm there. The property remained in the family until 1986 when it was sold to Leo O'Brien.

From his diaries, Connie Chapman Dumas surmises that her grandfather, Paul Chapman, worked in Pennsylvania and Illinois for Westinghouse testing electrical meters for companies. Her grandmother was from Iowa, and they were married October 30, 1914. "He came back and took over the farm when my great grandfather, Marvin Wright Chapman died," writes Dumas. When the farm was deeded to Paul Chapman on July 14, 1920, it consisted of 336 acres in Williston and Jericho.

Connie Chapman Dumas describes the farm house this way from back to front.

> *The cheese house was moved about 1948 when the tenant house burned the winter before from a chimney fire. Dark roof was the summer kitchen*

Mary S. Wright Chapman married George Adams Chapman on March 17, 1836. George was the first Chapman to settle in North Williston. *Courtesy of Connie Chapman Dumas.*

*area that burned, attributed to my Aunt Barbara playing with matches, it must have been sometime in the mid-1930s. The main house was where I was brought up.*

*It's a plank house. Thus, according to my folks, impossible to update, instead of insulation in the walls, it has planks. Upstairs were wide pine plank floors. Wearing spike heels in the 1960s drove my folks crazy at it marked up the floors. Until I was in high school, we had a coal furnace with*

Marvin W. Chapman and his second wife, Lucia Johnson Chapman. The photo was taken before 1884. *Courtesy of Connie Chapman Dumas.*

Blanche and Lucian Paul Chapman in the early 1930s. *Courtesy of Connie Chapman Dumas.*

An early view of the Chapman farm, looking north toward Saxon Hill in Essex. *Courtesy of Connie Chapman Dumas.*

The Chapman farm house. *Courtesy of Connie Chapman Dumas.*

*steam radiators, started only in late October, as it was too hard to control if any warming occurred. So the first cold days of the fall we huddled in the kitchen, where one end of the gas stove had a wood burning section.*

Architectural historian Jan Lewandowski states plank houses were constructed of sawn planks one and one-half to four inches thick, with a width of nine to twenty-six inches. The planks were placed vertically and often pegged together and attached to the sill and plate of the building. This could replace all or part of the internal framework of the house and gave the builder an exterior surface and an interior wall that could take the desired finish. This type of construction was popular in northern New England from 1790 to 1830.

The Chapman house was moved on September 2, 1994 to become the home of the Daniel and Ellen Fontaine family at 255 Chapman Lane. During the Fontaine's renovation the challenges of plank construction were once again evident.

Farmers were always looking for a way to bring in extra income. Lucian Paul Chapman cut pulp logs in 1923 and probably shipped them by rail to

The Chapman log slide built to remove pulp wood from the water. *Courtesy of Connie Chapman Dumas.*

the International Paper plant in Milton. The plant was located at the Great Falls of the Lamoille River. It started operations in June of 1899, and it was closed by a strike in 1925 and never reopened. Chapman's diary tells us about the challenges of pulp log cutting on the farm.

> *Tuesday, August 21*
> *We built our log slide and put it in the river.*
>
> *Wednesday, August 22*
> *We began to put logs in the river. Had some trouble skidding as the logs were pretty large for Ned* [the horse] *to handle.*
>
> *Thursday, August 23*
> *Tried out our slide this morning and it worked fine. Ned on the rope and me had plenty of power. We skidded logs with Neddie and got along better than yesterday.*
>
> *Wednesday, September 5, 1923*
> *Pulling logs out of the river.*
>
> *Thursday, September 6, 1923*
> *Sawing logs and skidding to the river.*
>
> *Friday, November 2, 1923*
> *Husking corn in the sheep barn. Put the young stock in the barn. Got news from Int. Paper Co. that they did not want to buy my pulp. Have to look now for some other market.*
>
> *Saturday, December 1, 1923*
> *Water up this morning. We had to use the boat to get over to the pulp wood. If it had risen 3 feet higher it would have taken our wood off. Pretty close shave. We sawed up about two cords today. Water going down tonight.*

Part of the Chapman land was utilized in a much different fashion starting in 1960. In the fall of that year Williston residents Howard Carpenter and Arthur Tuthill were looking for a spot to build a small ski area. The Chapman property, with its north-facing hill, was a logical location, and with the agreement of Bob and Peg Chapman, the project was soon underway. Besides Carpenter, Tuthill and Chapman, the Williston Ski Associates included Len Mercia, Charles Pillsbury, Marvin Clark, John Lantman, Herb Painter and Dave Yandell. The hill was rigged with a rope tow powered by a rusty Chevy, and by Christmas, the slope was open. It served the community with a Saturday afternoon ski school for many years and is now part of the Fontaine property.

## Fay Lane

The history of Fay Lane is more complicated, with its connections to Redmond Road and Old Stage Road. On July 9, 1861, seven men petitioned the selectboard of Williston for a road to lead from "the dwelling house now occupied by Theodor Cady… to some point on the Highway leading from Winooski River to Williston Village by the Vermont Central Rail Road Depot." The petition was approved on August 16, 1862, with the conditions that it would be a "Pent Road" with several "Gates or Bars" between the property owners along the road. The gates would allow cattle to roam from one side of the road to the other but kept stock from adjacent farms separate. Travelers would have to stop, open a gate and close it behind them as they progressed. By Vermont law, residents can still request permission from the selectboard to establish a pent road, now generally limited to class IV roads and trails.

The June 2, 1870 petition called for the establishment of a road from the current end of Fay Lane, or the then Murray Fay house, to head west, paralleling the railroad tracks, to the house of Daniel Shehan located on the river. Then it was to run south to the George Osborn(e) property on the current Redmond Road. This was an attempt to extend Fay Lane and connect it with the current Redmond Road as a town highway. It was turned down by the selectmen, "The public good and convenience…will not warrant the opening of a road and the expense necessary to work it and therefore the prayer of the petitioners should not be granted." Eventually this approximate route was approved as a town highway, as witnessed by the fact that Fay Lane was called Redmond Road well into the 1970s. "No [original road] survey was found for the section of road between Redmond Road and Old Stage Road and the Fay Lane Intersection," according to Gauthier's ancient roads research.

On April 29, 1871, the official survey in chains and links for the current Fay Lane was approved by selectmen George Morton, Hiram Walston and Lewis H. Talcott.

Fay Lane headed west from North Williston Road and connected with Old Stage Road, according to the 1857 Walling map and the 1869 Beers map. A discontinuance for this section was issued by the town in 1952. On the 1915 Sanborn insurance map, Fay Lane is marked as School Street since it was the location of the North Williston school built in 1864.

A ghost story connected to Fay Lane was recounted in the Chittenden County Historical Society's *Look Around Essex and Williston, Vermont*. The Forant family, residents of Fay Lane, owned race horses. After the parents died, the children were to place appropriate monuments on their graves. The promise was not carried out, so the ghosts of the horses could be heard racing up and down the road and into the barn. Only after the headstones were bought and placed on the graves were the sounds of racing horses silenced forever.

Today, Chapman Lane and Fay Lane are roads with no outlets.

## The Fay Family

The Fay name predominates on the 1869 Beers inset map of North Williston, where they conducted business and farmed. In addition, the children of John and Polly Fay of Richmond, Vermont, were connected through marriage or direct ancestry to other North Williston families, such as the Browns, Wrights and Whitcombs. The John M. Fay (J.M. Fay) house was on what is now Fay Lane. The Hiram J. Fay (H.J. Fay) house is now 2588 North Williston Road, and the Roswell B. Fay (R.B. Fay) house is at 2738 North Williston Road by the river. There are also a number of businesses owned by Hiram J. Fay noted, including the rake factory, the mill and a machine shop. In addition, there is a house near the Chapman farm in the lower right hand corner owned by Hiram.

Roswell B. Fay was born in Richmond, Vermont, on July 5, 1808, the oldest child of John and Polly. He moved to Williston in 1838 with his wife, Ann, and took up farming and lumber manufacturing. By 1860, Roswell's parents had joined the household. Roswell and Ann had five children: Marcia Eliza, John Miles, Alfred Cutler, Cynthia Roxana and Lucy Valera.

Fay served as a representative from the town in the Vermont State Assembly and as judge for probate. He was very involved in the building of the Universalist church in Williston that now serves as the town hall. In 1886, at age seventy-seven, he moved to the Oakland, California area where his daughter Cynthia and son Alfred C. lived. Cynthia was married to Alameda County supervisor Jonathan R. Talcott, former North Williston storekeeper and postmaster, and Alfred was a dairy farmer. Fay died there on August 25, 1905, at the age of ninety-seven. He was buried in the East Cemetery in Williston.

## HIRAM J. FAY AND THE PRODUCTION OF HAY RAKES

Roswell's brother, Hiram J. Fay, born on Christmas in 1831, was the youngest child of John and Polly. He was heavily involved in the businesses in North Williston. Perhaps the most interesting was the manufacturing of horse-drawn hay rakes designed by C.W. Warner.

Warner of New Haven, Vermont, in his patent letter of August 18, 1868, claimed to have "invented a new and useful Improvement in Horse Hay-Rakes." These rakes had revolving rake heads and projecting teeth in opposite directions. Warner said, with his invention, the rake head could be unlocked, and the initial revolution could be done with one movement by the operator. The rake also could easily fold on the carriage when transported. These features were the basis of his patent, number 81,234.

The American Institute of the City of New York 1869 report said, "It works easily, is readily transported, and is not readily broken, and can be repaired on the farm."

In another testimonial, Harmon Northrop of Fairfield, Vermont, wrote to the *New England Farmer* on June 15, 1868: "After trying several kinds of rakes, I have used for the last three years one of the Warner wooden revolving rakes, attached to wheels…it rakes clean, makes the snuggest window (*sic*), and the best to pitch of any that I ever saw, except those made with a hand rake. They are easily managed, and durable. The rakes are manufactured at Williston, Vermont."

The long teeth on the revolving rake were pulled flat along the ground, where they gathered the hay. When the rake was full of hay, the farmer would pull the handle, and the leading teeth would set into the ground, causing the rake to flip over, dump the collected hay and repeat the process with what had been the trailing teeth. The hay was deposited in windrows that stretched across the field.

*The Vermont Farm Year In 1890* states the hay rake was known as a "Shin Breaker" because of what it could do to the operator, and it was certainly a product of "America's Wood Age." The revolving horse-drawn rake was

Illustration from the *Report of the Iowa State Agricultural Society for the Year 1867*, page 225. *Courtesy of University of Vermont Special Collections.*

Marvin "Bob" Chapman and Ned the horse hitched to a dump rake in 1926. *Courtesy of Connie Chapman Dumas.*

part of the mechanization of agriculture, and its output equaled that of five men using hand rakes.

The caption accompanying the drawing of the Warner rake in the Iowa report said it was durable "and not liable to get out of order. It is completely under the control of the operator, and so easy in its working that a boy can manage it." It was praised "first, because it gathers the hay free from dust and sand; second, it closes the winrow (*sic*) in good shape for pitching; third, is made of wood, and a break can readily be repaired."

In spite of these endorsements, Hiram Fay's rake manufacturing was apparently a short-lived business because it is listed in *Walton's Vermont Register and Farmer's Almanac* for just one year, 1869.

The time of the revolving horse-drawn rake was coming to an end when Fay started to manufacture them. The first models appeared before 1820 and were popular until after the Civil War, when they were replaced by lighter, more efficient dump rakes. These rakes, according to Allen R. Yale Jr. in *While the Sun Shines, Making Hay in Vermont, 1789–1990*, could "do the work of eight to ten men raking by hand."

## THE NORTH WILLISTON MILL COMPANY

There is no agreement in the historical record on the exact dates for the establishment of the sawmill and gristmill in North Williston. Graffagnino states Hiram J. Fay started the steam sawmill in 1862. A newspaper article written after the 1871 fire says the sawmill was established in 1865 and the gristmill in 1869. The R.B. Fay and Company saw- and gristmills are listed in the 1867 *Walton's Register*.

Regardless of the specific year in which the mills opened, in 1866, Roswell B. Fay and Almon Rood joined the business.

The *Daily Free Press and Times* of Burlington reported on the fire at the mills on September 16, 1871:

> *The steam saw mill and grist mill of H.J. Fay at North Williston were destroyed by fire last night. The fire was discovered about 10 o'clock p.m. in the engine room of the saw mill. The building and contents are a total loss, with exception of a small quantity of grain which was saved from the grist mill. The saw mill was built in 1865, and the grist mill in 1869. Loss $30,000. Mr. Fay was insured for $17,000. The second story of the saw mill was occupied by Stevens & Marrs, manufacturer of doors,*

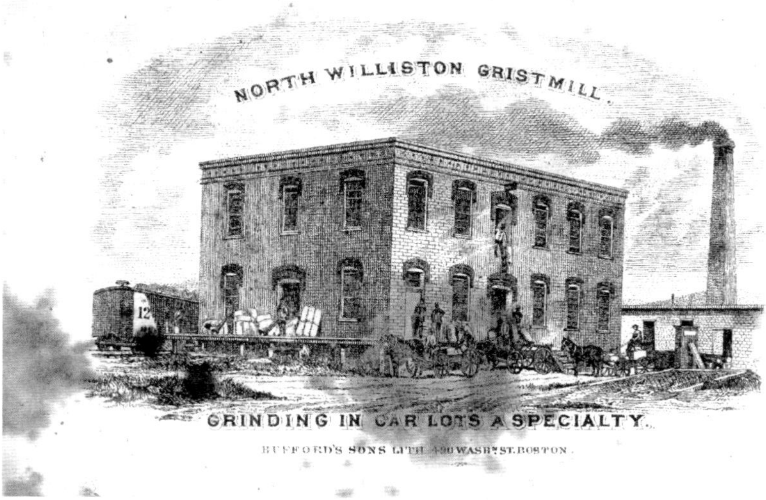


On the reverse side of this business card from the 1870s, J.R. Talcott is noted as the proprietor of the gristmill and the storekeeper in North Williston. *Courtesy of Williston Historical Society.*

> *sash and blinds, who had just put in new machinery. Loss $2,500, insured for $1,200. The above insurance was obtained through the office of S. and R.S. Wires of this city.*

The North Williston Mill Company grew from the ashes. The brick mill building depicted on the J.R. Talcott business card replaced the original mill destroyed by the 1871 fire. Talcott ran the North Williston general store and was postmaster from 1873 to 1879.

From J. Kevin Graffagnino's research on a chronology of North Williston businesses, we learn that, in 1876, John Whitcomb joined North Williston Mill Company, and the name was changed to Whitcomb & Fay, a gristmill and lumber business. A Whitcomb & Fay invoice dated August 9, 1880, made out to Smith Wright lists mill feed, dimension lumber, shingles, clapboards and posts as products of the industry.

## John Whitcomb

John Whitcomb was born on December 13, 1820 in Richmond, Vermont. He was the eighth of fifteen children of Thomas and Anna (Steven) Whitcomb. He married into the Fay family. The 1886 W.S. Rann *History of Chittenden*

John Whitcomb (1820–1903). Drawing from Rann's *History of Chittenden County*.

*County Vermont* provides some details of his life. He worked on his brother's farm in Essex and then headed west. He drove cattle across the plains and dealt with Indians and "wild beasts." He came down with smallpox and typhoid fever and returned to Vermont to regain his health. In 1860, he married Edith Fay, the youngest daughter of John Fay, who lived in North Williston on what later became the Fontaine farm (2738 North Williston Road). John Fay's youngest child, Hiram, would become John Whitcomb's partner in the mill business.

In 1869, Whitcomb headed west again, this time to Sacramento, California. He established a ranch of 4,200 acres, with 600 cattle, 300 milkers, 65 horses and 4,200 sheep. He also raised grain. He stayed there six years and then came back to Williston and purchased the farm from his brother-in-law, Hiram J. Fay. He eventually owned farms in Jericho, Essex and Waterbury for a total of 1,250 acres in Vermont. Along with his Vermont property, Whitcomb had 500 acres on Valcour Island, New York; 2,400 acres in Kansas; and 2,000 head of cattle in Wyoming. Whitcomb represented Williston in the state House of Representatives in 1892.

John and Edith Fay Whitcomb had one daughter, Marcia Fay Whitcomb, born May 4, 1861, who married James Kennedy. Julia (Mentzer) Fifield's parents bought their North Williston house from James and Marcia Kennedy.

From 1879 to 1894, Whitcomb was the North Williston storekeeper and postmaster. The Hamilton Child *Gazetteer and Business Directory of Chittenden County, Vermont For 1882–1883* describes him as a "dealer in dry goods, groceries and provisions, hats, caps, trunks, boots, shoes and rubbers, notions, etc."

John Whitcomb died on July 18, 1903, owning a great deal of property worth $65,780. His estate inventory totaled $108,991, all left to his only child, Marcia Kennedy. That total was more than double Smith Wright's estate of $53,751.50, making Whitcomb perhaps the wealthiest man in Williston at the time.

With the death of John Whitcomb, the lumber and shingle business was discontinued. The gristmill had several owners until Roswell E. Brown assumed control in 1913. It continued to 1934 as one of the longer lasting businesses in North Williston.

As to the fate of the mill building, Albert Fontaine, in *La Famille Fontaine*, written in 1984, states that "from 1936 to 1940 this building was owned by Arthur Yandow, Sr. and his brother Fred Yandow. They operated their grain business [here]...The building and lot were purchased from Beatrice Fontaine Yandow (widow of Arthur) in 1960 by her father, Euclide Fontaine. The building was demolished and the land went with the Fontaine farm."

The Fay family line can be traced from Roswell B. to his son, John M., and then to his son, Harry Martin Fay. The last of the Fays on Fay Lane were Harry and his wife, Josie. Harry was a farmer, and besides the two years spent in California, he served in the Vermont legislature and as a Williston selectman, lister, justice of the peace and auditor. Josie Fay was one of the first women to serve in the legislature after the passage of the Nineteenth Amendment in 1920.

The John M. Fay/Harry Fay house on Fay Lane. *Courtesy of Williston Historical Society, Talcott album.*

The Fay house on Fay Lane was built circa 1858. When it burned in 1938, it was occupied by Josie, widow of Harry, who had died on January 6, 1930. The house was located on the south side of the road past the school house.

The fire was reported in the September 8, 1938 *Suburban List* this way:

> *Fire of unknown origin destroyed the home known as the Harry Fay place in North Williston Sunday morning about 1:30. This was one of the older dwellings in this section, being about 80 years old, built by Hiram Fay. It was a wooden, two-story house, with long ell adjoining and was much admired for its simple beauty.*
>
> *The Essex Junction fire department was called and remained until 7 in the morning, when the danger of the barns burning had passed. It is reported the fire was discovered by the troupe who had presented the "Winter Garden Revue" at the fair, each day during the last week. They were motoring to Lewiston, Me., from the Chapin House, on the Jericho road, where they had been guests the past week. They saw the flames flashing from the Fay House and stopped to arouse the occupants. They remained to rescue what they could of the furniture, some of which, owned by Mrs. Josie Fay Greene, are valuable antiques. The other occupants, the Walter Doenges, who purchased the farm about a year ago, lost most of their furniture and belongings. The loss is considered over $5,000. Although to rebuild the*

> *house would probably cost twice that. The loss, it is understood, is partially covered by insurance. This is one of the very fertile valley farms which border the river and consists of 250 aces, tying 50 head. Mrs. Fay Greene was taken Sunday morning to the home of Mrs. Paul Chapman and later brought to the home of Mr. and Mrs. W.J. Francis in Essex Junction.*

Today, the Chapman and Fay families are remembered by the two side roads of North Williston. The Landvater place has replaced the Chapman farm, and the North Williston Cattle Company, operated by the Whitcomb family, uses land formerly owned by the Fay family. The bottom land along the Winooski River remains true to its agricultural roots.

## *Chapter 12*

# Down Depot Hill

## *North Williston Road*

North Williston Road runs north–south and connects Williston Road in the village of Williston with River Road (Route 117) in Essex. It is very easy to travel the length of the nearly three-mile road at thirty-five miles per hour and not know you have passed through an historic section of Williston.

Charles Lewis Heyde (1820–1892) was a landscape artist in the Hudson River School tradition. He devoted nearly forty years of his life to mainly painting scenes in Vermont, such as his depiction of North Williston.

William C. Lipke, in *Charles Louis Heyde: Nineteenth-Century Vermont Landscape Painter*, says this about the North Williston scene.

> [It] *documents even more dramatically the clearing of the forested wilderness, the impact of settlement, and the arrival of the 'machine in the garden,' in this case the newly opened (1849) railroad as it steams toward Burlington. Here Mount Mansfield is displaced—literally set aside—as the focal point of the composition by the changing and modified landscape that is the result of increased settlement: forests have been converted into useful pastureland, and the built environment encroaches upon what once was wilderness.*

North Williston Road originally took a more direct route to the river than what exists today. As one travels on the road headed north and is about to descend into the woods and through the curves to North Williston, Peterson Lane appears straight ahead. This lane, still a town highway, indicates the

The earliest view of what would become North Williston Road, an 1856 painting of North Williston by Charles Louis Heyde. © *Shelburne Museum, Shelburne, Vermont.*

straight routing of the original North Williston Road. It continued across the current Perkins property and then descended steeply north toward the river. Traces of the old road are still visible today. John Johnson drew up a map circa 1820, to settle the estate of Giles Chittenden, that depicted the straight route of North Williston Road from the now Governor Chittenden Road to the Onion (Winooski) River.

According to the Williston Road Record Book, Volume 1, the road commissioners of Chittenden County were petitioned on August 12, 1829, to reroute the road down the hill and, in addition, establish it as a county highway through Essex to Jericho Four Corners, currently where Route 15 intersects with Lee River Road and Plains Road. The commissioners notified the interested parties, including the selectmen of Williston, Essex and Jericho, of a meeting at 9:00 a.m. on September 23 at the Eagle Tavern in Williston to consider the issue. Apparently the Jericho selectmen didn't show up, but "after due examination and full consideration [the attending commissioners] unanimously agree[d] that the said road shall be laid and altered."

What follows in the record of that meeting is a detailed description of the new route in "the valley or ravine," with compass headings and chain/link measurements until it reached the previously established "traveled road on the West side of a small conical eminence, surrounded by the flat ground." This rerouting gave North Williston Road the current path that swings to the west as it curves through the woods today. It furnished a much more gradual grade compared to the original route.

Dr. Oscar S. Peterson Jr. moved to Williston in 1944 into a house at 25 Peterson Lane. Peterson, in his research and writing of Williston history, adds the following to the historical record.

> [Authors] *Moody and Putnam note that oral tradition places the original course as an extension of Peterson Lane. Remnants of a very old graded road can be faintly traced five or six rods east of and parallel with Peterson Lane. Beside it is a partially filled cellar hole near the crest of a rise. Mrs. Olive O'Brien, in a conversation with* [Dr. Peterson and his wife, Jeneva] *in the mid-1940s, told of a log house which stood here when she was young. The course of this old road and its extension, still partly traceable to its joining with North Williston Road near the Glenn Emery home* [2096 North Williston Road] *fits more closely the highway depicted…on* [early maps] *than does the present gulley route.*

Henry Tarrier made this comment on the original North Williston Road during the 1990 North Williston Oral History Night: "It went from Dr. Peterson's right down the hill to Emery's. But it was awful steep. The road was showing twenty years ago. You could see that road all the way down."

After crossing the river, the road was to connect to the present Route 117. It then headed west, turned north to pass on the west side of Saxon Hill, using the route of the present Saxon Hill Road, and then turned east to Jericho on the now Route 15.

The ruling by the commissioners decreed that the road should be open for travel "by the first day of November…1831, except the Bridge across Onion River, about which no order is made." Pointing out the bridge issue, the commissioners were perhaps dropping a strong hint that the ferry service was inadequate, and it was time to consider the logical alternative.

From the Williston land records, the name changes for the road over the years reflect interesting milestones in Williston's history. In the early 1800s, it was the "road leading from the village to Onion River."

In 1832, it is noted as the "road leading from Tremont Hotel to Thompson's (*sic*) Ferry." Today's Williston Road through the village was preceded by the Winooski Turnpike, established in 1805, that connected Burlington and Montpelier. Williston had several taverns that served as stops on the turnpike. The Tremont Hotel is not listed in John C. Wriston's *Vermont Inns & Taverns*, but it may have been the Eagle Hall/Tavern renamed, located on the northeast section of the four corners in the village of Williston. Thomson's cable ferry across the Winooski River used Chapman property to connect with Jericho. In 1836 it is referred to as the "road leading from Eagle Hall to Chittenden's Ferry."

## The Proposed Plank Road

One version of North Williston Road was never built. The Williston and Jericho Plank Road Company was incorporated by the Vermont General Assembly on November 11, 1850, with a capital stock of $10,000 "for the purpose and with the right of building a plank road with a single or double track from the Winooski Turnpike at Eagle Hall in Williston in the county of Chittenden upon the nearest route to the Four Corners so called in Jericho… for persons and teams to pass and repass." This was just about a year after the arrival of the rails in Williston and was one of fourteen plank roads incorporated in Vermont.

A plank road was built as an effort to deal with the perennial problem of poor drainage, mud and ruts that plagued dirt roads. The road grant was four rods (sixty-six feet) wide and was supposed to be under construction within three years. The first toll gate could not be erected until at least one-half of the distance of the road was complete.

Roswell B. Fay's North Williston homestead was right at the point where the road would have crossed the river, giving him a personal interest in the project.

The plank road would have connected farmers and others needing access to rail transportation to the North Williston depot.

Daniel B. Klein and John Majewski, in their article "Turnpikes and Toll Roads in Nineteenth-Century America," describe the construction of plank roads this way: "Road builders put down two parallel lines of timbers four or five feet apart, which formed the 'foundation' of the road. They then laid, at right angles, planks that were about eight feet long and three or four inches thick. Builders used no nails or glue to secure the planks—they were secured only by their own weight—but they did build ditches on each side of the road to insure proper drainage."

Civil engineer George Geddes, from the Syracuse, New York area, oversold plank roads. In a *Scientific American* article cited by Klein and Majewski, Geddes underestimated the cost and life expectancy of plank roads. He said the plank roads in Toronto would last eight years, but actually four or five years was more realistic.

Klein and Majewski suggest—for the appointed Williston plank road commissioners David French, David A. Murray, Fay and Truman Galusha and John H. Tower of Jericho—that the motivation to build such a road was probably less about a return on a personal investment and more from the "convenience and increased trade and development that the roads would bring." Given the short actual life of a plank road, the era was brief, lasting from 1847 to 1853.

North Williston Road was described as "leading from Eagle Hall to the depot," after the railroad came through North Williston in 1849. Eagle Hall burned down in 1850, and from about 1869 on, the road was "leading from Methodist Church to the depot." The large white church on the corner of North Williston Road and Williston Road was built as a Methodist church and dedicated on October 6, 1869. The Williston Federated Church was born in 1899 when the Congregational church agreed to join with the Methodists.

William Burnett was paid $100 "for macadamizing depot road," according to the 1880 Williston town report. This involved several layers of crushed stones, with the largest on the bottom covered with increasingly smaller stones to eventually attain a fairly hard smooth surface. It was certainly an improvement over a dirt road, but macadam had its own problems with dust and mud.

Locals called the route Depot Road for many years, and travel on it could be hazardous or fun, depending upon the mode of transportation and the

North Williston postcard from 1909. Depot Road is left of center; Bean Hill is on the left; Saxon Hill in Essex forms the distant horizon. *Courtesy of Gertrude Gonyo.*

season. Depot Road was the route the stage took from North Williston to the village several times a day, transporting mail and passengers.

In the winter, the road could provide a great trip on a sled. Gertrude Urie lived in a farm house on the corner of Mountain View Road and North Williston Road:

> *In my childhood days we didn't have lots of warm clothes; ours were always made-overs. But we sometimes would dress in Pop's long underwear and heavy pants and walk to the top of North Williston Hill—then it was Depot Hill—and slide to the railroad tracks. We'd go down two deep—one lay down on the sled and the other on top, carrying a lighted flashlight. If we saw car lights, we'd ditch ourselves. What a time we'd have getting out of the bank and then getting the light way down in the snow. We usually made three or four trips before trudging home.*

Gertrude Gonyo also enjoyed sliding on Depot Hill: "I remember that as a kid we liked to slide, like all children do, and to show you how little traffic came down to North Williston, we staged somebody at the top of North Williston hill where the Petersons live, and watched to see if there might be a car or two, and the rest of us slid down that whole hill all the way to the railroad track."

Winter scene on Depot Road (Main Street) in the early 1900s. Looking north, the house at 2361 North Williston Road is on the left. *Courtesy of Williston Historical Society.*

Henry Tarrier recalls one of the challenges of traveling on Depot Road: "When I was a kid, when you went down Depot Hill in the summer time you tied a handkerchief across your face because the sand was blowing across." Newspaper clippings from the 1920s often mentioned "sandblows" in several parts of town, probably the result of deforestation and poor farming techniques.

Julia (Mentzer) Fifield remembers a similar experience traveling south to Williston on Depot Road: "I want to tell you, in the winter, the snow that blew across there was enough to make you cringe. There wasn't a tree, from the turn until you pass the Stovepipe Corners. Not a tree, not a tree. There were one or two trees in the farm that you met there, right by the house, but not in the plain…Not as far as you could look this way and that way."

The Smith Wright Company used a horse to raise ice to the second floor of the cold storage building. One of Fifield's favorite trips on Depot Road was when she was charged with taking the horse to the blacksmith shop in Williston. It was "the most beautiful grey Percheron you ever looked at… with a great wide back." As Fifield rode the horse to Williston "to be shod," she would "collect all the kids all the way up. We'd go up about five of us on the back of this horse." The blacksmith shop was located on the west side of North Williston Road across from the Federated church, where the parking lot is now.

The bandstand at the intersection of Depot Road, coming in from the left, with Williston Road in the center. *Courtesy of University of Vermont Special Collections.*

Two North Williston boys, Charles Irish and Bob Chapman, along with some friends, traveled on Depot Road with a different destination in mind. There was a bandstand that stood at the intersection of Depot Road and Williston Road. It seems as a Halloween prank they would move the bandstand by tipping it on its side and rolling it out of sight. When asked if he ever got in trouble for this, Charles Irish replied, "No, I wouldn't say I really got in trouble. Didn't get caught. That's a good way to put it."

The 1940 town report lists the black top for North Williston Road costing over $4,100, paid mostly by the state. It was a multiyear project; the black topping was finished to the North Williston bridge in 1942.

Today, North Williston Road serves as an access to the village of Williston from the north, feeding traffic into the intersection with Oak Hill Road and Williston Road in the heart of the village. The historic nature of the intersection has been brought to the forefront in light of the proposed roundabout to improve the safety of motorists and pedestrians. Most recently, a roundabout is under consideration for the intersection of North Williston, Mountain View and Governor Chittenden Roads.

# Afterword

North Williston, a post village and station on the Vermont Central Railroad, located in the northwestern part, contains a store, schoolhouse, cheese factory, blacksmith shop, machine shop, etc., and about twenty dwellings," according to the 1882 *Gazetteer and Business Directory of Chittenden County, Vermont*. What is it today?

North Williston, like the village of Williston, and the area around Taft Corners grew mainly because of a transportation system. Besides the railroad, the road network of the state has impacted Williston's economy and growth more than once. Early in the 1800s, Williston's location on the main route between Burlington and Montpelier—the Winooski Turnpike—led to the establishment of several taverns and stores in town. In the 1960s, the interstate split Williston into northern and southern sections. Today, the interchange at Route 2A and the area around Taft Corners have become a major commercial center in part due to its proximity to I-89.

Today, Williston is a town of contrasts. Author Jan Albers decries the present look of the section of Williston around Taft Corners as "strangely disorienting" with "dizzying boulevards" among the box stores. This is in contrast to the village with "elegant white clapboard houses and distinguished public buildings arrayed prettily along the old road."

She does not comment on the appearance of North Williston.

Unlike Taft Corners and the western sections of Williston, North Williston has not been engulfed by the spread of suburbia outside of Burlington and Essex Junction. The geographic isolation of North Williston is maintained by its distance from the interstate highway, the barrier of the Winooski River and its flood cycles and its location on a secondary road.

North Williston is in an Agriculture/Rural Residential Zoning District, which means "the uses permitted...are limited to agriculture, the production of forest products, the mining or quarrying of nonmetallic minerals, outdoor education and recreation, and residential development that results in substantial open space conservation," according to the Unified Development Bylaw for the Town of Williston. Another limiting factor is the classification of much of the land as flood plain.

Given the existence of the North Williston Historic District and the 2007 proposal from the zoning and planning department to establish a local historic district that would extend the boundary of the state designated district, questions arise about the proper focus of such entities. Since North Williston was primarily an industrial and agricultural section of town, what should be the focus of a historic district there? In light of the fires and demolition of other buildings, what historic preservation is worth instituting? The North Williston Historic District survey states "[b]ecause of the concentration of industry that existed for such a defined time, the strip along either side of Chapman Lane is archeologically sensitive." Should this area undergo proper archaeological surveying?

Current resident Marianne Riordan draws this parallel between North Williston of yesterday and today. "Life here in North Williston may likely be a modern version of what it was like for the folks who first settled here. Families are still working the earth, the neighborhood kids are still getting together to play out-of-doors in the fields and woods, and the old houses are still providing shelter from Mother Nature."

North Williston today is a unique Williston neighborhood, with historic homes, the school building, the railroad tracks and a few foundations serving as reminders of the busy place it was in the late 1800s and early 1900s. Given Williston's reputation for preserving its history, especially through the Williston Historical Society and the town plan, the history of this section of the town is secure.

# Selected Bibliography


*Acts and Resolves Passed by the General Assembly of the State of Vermont. No. 108, An Act to Incorporate the Williston and Jericho Plank Road Company, November 11, 1850*. Montpelier, VT: E.P Walton & Son, 1852.

Albers, Jan. *Hands on the Land: A History of the Vermont Landscape*. Cambridge, MA: MIT Press, 2000.

Allen, Richard H. *The History of Williston Central School: 1950 to 2000*. Milton, VT: Villanti & Sons, 2001.

Anderson, Oscar Edward Jr. *Refrigeration in American: A History of a New Technology and Its Impact*. Princeton, NJ: Princeton University Press, 1953.

*Annual Report of the Iowa State Agricultural Society for the Year 1867*. Des Moines, IA: Society, 1868.

Arquit, Nora C. Harris. *Before My Own Time and Since 1513–1978, Genealogy of the Harris Family, 1513-1978, Their Allied Families, with Historical Sketches and Illustrations of the Places They Lived and Worked in Europe and America*. Ithaca, NY: self published, 1978.

Bathory-Kitz, Dennis. *A History and Guide: Country Stores of Vermont*. Charleston, SC: The History Press, 2008.

Beck, Jane C. *The General Store in Vermont: An Oral History*. Middlebury, VT: Vermont Folklife Center, 1988.

Beers, F.W. *Atlas of Chittenden County, Vermont*. Rutland, VT: Charles E. Tuttle Company, 1971. First published in 1869.

Bellerose, George. "Williston's Chicken Pie Suppers." *Vermont Life* (Autumn 1981).

Bent, Frank, ed. *The History of Essex, Vermont*. Essex, VT: Essex Publishing Company, 1963.

Bigelow, Walter J. *Vermont, Its Government.* Montpelier, VT: Historical Publishing Company, 1919–1933.

Blow, David. *Historic Guide to Burlington Neighborhoods, Vol. II.* Burlington, VT: Queen City Printers, 1997.

Carleton, Hiram. *Genealogical and Family History of the State of Vermont, Vols. I and II.* New York: Lewis Publishing, 1903.

Carlisle, Lilian Baker, ed. *Look Around Colchester and Milton, Vermont.* Burlington, VT: George Little Press, Inc., 1975.

———. *Look Around Essex and Williston, Vermont.* Burlington, VT: George Little Press, Inc., 1973.

———. *Look Around St. George and Shelburne, Vermont.* Burlington, VT: George Little Press, Inc., 1975.

Child, Hamilton, ed. *Gazetteer and Business Directory of Chittenden County for 1882–1883*. Syracuse, NY: Journal Office, 1882.

Clark, Erwin S. *History of the Town of Addison, 1609–1976*. Middlebury, VT: Addison Press Inc., 1976.

Clifford, Deborah Pickman, and Nicholas R. Clifford. *The Troubled Roar of the Waters: Vermont in Flood and Recovery, 1927–1931*. Durham: University of New Hampshire Press, 2007.

Cooley, Oscar. *When Grandpa Was a Boy.* Montpelier: Vermont Historical Society, 1985.

Cooper, Madison. *Practical Cold Storage: The Theory, Design, and Construction of Buildings and Apparatus for the Preservation of Perishable Products, Approved Methods of Applying Refrigeration and the Care and Handling of Eggs, Fruit, Dairy Products, etc.* Chicago, IL: Nickerson & Collins Co., 1905.

Dean, Carol. *The History of Schools in Williston, Vermont*. Williston, VT: self published, 1992.

Duffy, John J., Samuel B. Hand and Ralph H. Orth. *The Vermont Encyclopedia*. Lebanon, NH: University Press of New England, 2003.

Fish, Charles. *In the Land of the Wild Onion: Travels Along Vermont's Winooski River*. Burlington, VT, Hanover, NH, and London: University of Vermont Press and University Press of New England, 2006.

Fontaine, Albert. *La Famille Fontaine.* N.p., 1984.

Friedman, Walter A. *Birth of a Salesman: The Transformation of Selling in America.* Cambridge, MA: Harvard University Press, 2004.

Gauthier, Ronald E. *Final Report Ancient Roads Research for the Town of Williston*. Williston, VT: Dubois & King, Inc., 2009.

Graff, Nancy Price, and E. Thomas Pierce, eds. *Charles Louis Heyde: Nineteenth-Century Vermont Landscape Painter.* Burlington: Robert Hull Fleming Museum, University of Vermont, 2001.

Graffagnino, J. Kevin. "North Williston, VT, 1850–1950." Unpublished manuscript, Dorothy Alling Memorial Library, Williston, Vermont, 1974.

Hastings, Scott E., Jr., and Geraldine S. Ames. *The Vermont Farm Year in 1890.* Woodstock, VT: Billings Farm and Museum, 1983.

Hayden, Chauncey H., Luther C. Stevens, LaFayette Wilbur and Rev. S.H. Barnum. *The History of Jericho, Vermont, Vol. I.* Burlington, VT: Free Press Printing Co. Printers and Binders, 1916.

The Historical Committee. *A History of the Town of Williston, 1763–1913.* N.p., 1913.

Jackson, Kathryn. *The Milton Story.* Burlington, VT: Burlington Vocational School, 1976. First published by the Milton Bicentennial Committee in 1963.

Johnson, John. *Map of Giles Chittenden Estate, c. 1820.* Special Collections, University of Vermont.

Jordan, Holman Drew. "Ten Vermont Towns: Social and Economic Characteristics, 1850–1870." PhD diss., University of Alabama, 1966. Copy in the Dorothy Alling Memorial Library, Williston, Vermont.

Klein, Daniel, and John Majewski. "Turnpikes and Toll Roads in Nineteenth-Century America." Edited by Robert Whaples. EH.Net Encyclopedia, http://eh.net/encyclopedia/article/Klein.Majewski.Turnpikes.

Lewandowski, Jan Leo. "The Plank Framed House in Northeastern Vermont." *Vermont History* 53 (Spring 1985): 104–121.

Lockwood, Glenn J. *Smiths Falls: A Social History of the Men and Women in a Rideau Canal Community, 1794–1994.* Carleton, Ontario: Motion Creative Printing, 1994.

MacArthur, Margaret. *Vermont Heritage Songs.* CD by Billy Shaw Soundesign, and Protosound, Inc. Vermont Folklife Center, 1994.

McLaughlin, Joseph, SSE. "The Limerick Lad, the Burlington Lady, and the Founding of Saint Michael's College." Paper presented at the third Burlington Irish Festival, March 16, 1998, http://www.cfd1.org/LIMERICK.pdf.

Merle, Elinor. *The History of Jericho, Vermont, Vol. II.* Burlington, VT: Queen City Printers, Inc., 1963.

Moody, F. Kennon, and Floyd D. Putnam. *The Williston Story.* Essex Junction, VT: Roscoe Printing House, 1961.

Painter, Ruth. "A Brief Look at Williston, Vermont in the 20s." *Williston Historical Society Bulletin* 16, no. 3 (July 1989).

Peterson, Oscar S., Jr. "A History of Williston, Governor Thomas Chittenden's Home Town." Unpublished manuscript, Dorothy Alling Memorial Library, Williston, Vermont.

Randall, Willard Sterne, and Nancy Nahra. *Thomas Chittenden's Town: A Story of Williston, Vermont*. Williston, VT: Williston Historical Society, 1998.

Rann, William S., ed. *History of Chittenden County Vermont with Illustrations and Biographical Sketches of Some of Its Prominent Men and Pioneers.* Syracuse, NY: D. Mason & Co, 1886.

Riggs, Harriet, ed., Julie Longstreth, Mary Ann McMaster, Betty Barney Preston, Heath K. Riggs, Ronald W. Rodjenski Jr., Neil Sherman, Frances Thomas, Peter A. Thomas and Martha Turner. *Richmond, Vermont: A History of More than 200 Years.* Burlington, VT: Queen City Printers, Inc. 2007.

Sanborn Map Company. *North Williston, Vermont*. June 1915. Special Collections, University of Vermont.

Sherman, Michael, Gene Sessions and P. Jeffrey Potash. *Freedom and Unity, A History of Vermont*. Barre: Vermont Historical Society, 2004.

Sundaram, Sivanuja S. "North Williston Bridge Historical Assessment." January 1991. Vermont Agency of Transportation, http://lcweb2.loc.gov/pnp/habshaer/vt/vt0100/vt0115/data/vt0115ascii.txt.

Walling, Henry F. *Map of Chittenden County Vermont from the Actual Surveys Under the Direction of H.F. Walling*. New York: Baker, Tilden & Co., 1858. Special Collections, University of Vermont.

Walton, E.P., ed. *Walton's Vermont Register and Farmer's Almanac*. Several publishers, 1819–1931.

Williston Historical Society. *North Williston Oral History Night.* Videotaped by Richard Allen. DVD reproduction by James R. Heltz of Green Mountain Video. Old Brick Church, Williston, Vermont, October 29, 1990. Copy in the Dorothy Alling Memorial Library, Williston, Vermont.

Wilson, Charles Morrow. "The Great Turkey Drive." *Vermont Life* (Autumn 1959).

———. *Postcards from Vermont, A Social History, 1905–1945*. Hanover, NH: New England Press, 2002.

Wilson, Harold Fisher. *The Hill Country of Northern New England: Its Social and Economic History, 1790–1930*. New York: AMS Press, Inc., 1967.

Wriston, John C., Jr. *Vermont Inns and Taverns, Pre-Revolution to 1925: An Illustrated and Annotated Checklist.* Rutland, VT: Academy Books, 1991.

Yale, Allen R., Jr. *While the Sun Shines, Making Hay in Vermont, 1789–1990.* Montpelier: Vermont Historical Society, 1991.

## Newspapers Consulted

*Burlington Clipper.*
*Burlington Daily Free Press and Times.*
*Burlington Daily News.*
*Burlington Free Press.*
*Burlington Free Press and Times.*
*Clarion* (Essex Junction, VT, High School newspaper).
*Essex Reporter.*
*Evening Tribune (Albert Lea, MN).*
*Suburban List (Essex Junction, VT).*
*Williston Observer.*
*Williston Whistle.*

## Other Records Consulted

Chittenden County (VT) probate records.
Diaries: Lucian Paul Chapman, Lucia Chapman, Lewis Talcott and George S. Talcott.
Interviews: Julia Fifield, Gertrude Gonyo, Connie Chapman Dumas, Gisele and Ellen Fontaine and Charles Irish.
John Forbes Scrapbook of newspaper clippings, Williston Historical Society collection.
Smith Wright family papers, University of Vermont Special Collections.
Town Records for Williston, St. George, Essex and Addison, Vermont.
U.S. censuses.

# Index

## D



## F



## G



## H



## I



## J



## K



## L



## M

## N



## P



## R



## S



## T



## U



## W



## Y

# About the Author

Richard H. Allen is a retired elementary school teacher with forty years of experience, including thirty-seven years in Williston. Allen coordinated many educational programs for the schools on local history. He is a lifetime member of the Williston Historical Society and a member of the Chittenden County Historical Society. He is the author or coauthor of several books, including *Our Town: Williston, VT*, *The Vermont Geography Book*, *The History of Williston Central School, 1950 to 2000* and *Essex and Essex Junction*.